A DISCOVERY GUIDE

LOOKING FOR FOSSILS

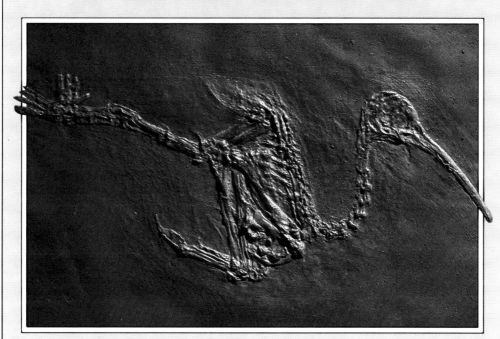

DR·DAVID·NORMAN

a Salamander book
Published by Salamander Books Limited
LONDON • NEW YORK

A SALAMANDER BOOK

Published by Salamander Books Ltd
129/137 York Way,
London N7 9LG,
United Kingdom.

Text © Dr David Norman 1990
Design © Salamander Books Ltd 1990

ISBN 0 86101 512 6

Distributed in the United Kingdom by
Hodder & Stoughton Services,
PO Box 6, Mill Road,
Dunton Green, Sevenoaks,
Kent TN13 2XX.

All correspondence concerning the content of this
volume should be addressed to the publishers.

CREDITS

Editor: Anne McDowall
Designer: Jill Coote
Line drawings: Peter Bull
© Salamander Books Ltd
Typesetting: Flairplan Phototypesetting Ltd
Colour separation: J Film, Singapore
Printed by: Proost International Book Production,
Turnout, Belgium

THE AUTHOR

David Norman is head of Palaeontology at the Nature Conservancy
Council of Great Britain and is responsible for the preservation of
Britain's most scientifically important palaeontological sites. In
addition, Dr Norman carries out scientific work as a research fellow
of the University Museum, Oxford. Dr Norman has made research
and collecting trips to many countries, including China, Romania,
Australia, USA, Canada and western Europe. He has written
numerous scientific articles and several books, including *The
Illustrated Encyclopedia of Dinosaurs* and *Dinosaurs* in the
Discovery Guide series, and has appeared on radio and television.

CONTENTS

INTRODUCTION

THE HISTORY OF THE EARTH

This book is first and foremost about fossils: what they are, how they formed, where to find them, how to collect them and what they can tell us about the history of life on Earth.

As we will see, fossils come in all shapes and sizes, from microscopically small – in the form of bacteria-like organisms measured in thousandths of a millimetre that are found in some of the most ancient rocks – to almost unbelievably big – some stupendously large dinosaurs, for example. It is not only organisms themselves that become fossilized; evidence of the presence or activities of organisms may also be preserved as fossils. *Trace fossils*, as they are called, include fossilized tracks or footprints, stomach stones, dung or even skin impressions.

The range of life that has been preserved in fossil form is quite remarkable, with representatives of all the Kingdoms of organisms known today, from bacteria and simple algae to single-celled organisms (such as are found in pond water), fungi, animals and plants. Fossils can be found in rocks that span over 3000 million years of Earth's history on every continent of the world: from the moist, tropical regions of Africa and the badlands of North America, to the rocky outcrops on the bleak and snowy wastes of Antarctica and the sandstone cliffs of the high, cold deserts of Mongolia.

Nevertheless, the variety of life represented by fossils is but a tiny sample of the enormous range of life that has existed throughout the long history of the Earth. The percentage of organisms living at any one time that will eventually become fossilized is very, very small. Fossilization is the exception rather than the rule: it depends upon a whole sequence of events occurring (see page 10), and if any of the elements in this sequence is lost (or interrupted), then so, too, is the potential fossil.

It should be obvious, therefore, that any fossil remains are of potentially great importance. Even an apparently trifling specimen forms part of an immense and complicated jigsaw puzzle that palaeontologists are grappling with in order to try and unravel the mysteries of the evolution of life. Looked at from this perspective, collecting fossils, amusing pastime though it can be, is also one that demands considerable care. Fossils are not an infinitely renewable resource, and should not be collected and discarded at will. They form part of our heritage, both nationally and internationally. (After all, our national boundaries, of which we are so aware in the present day, fade into insignificance when we consider the arrangements of the continents of the Earth over the billions of years of its history.)

Below: *The Colorado River has cut a huge gorge in the surface of the Earth: the Grand Canyon. Such layers of rock yield many fossils.*

The age of the Earth

Modern estimates of the age of the Earth – made possible by a scientific understanding of *radioactivity* (see *Glossary*, page 61) – suggest that it is in the region of 4600 million years old (which to us, who tend to measure things in terms of a human life of 80 years or so, is a simply incomprehensible span of time). Geologists have endeavoured to date different rocks, and by comparing the types of fossils each contains, to divide up this vast history of the Earth.

The major subdivisions in this geological timescale of the Earth are the three Eons: *Archaean,* the time of Earth history when no traces of life are found; *Proterozoic,* when only very simple forms of life (essentially single-celled organisms) existed; and *Phanerozoic,* which saw the evolution of larger, more obvious and more interesting forms of life. The boundaries between these Eons are somewhat arbitrary and are liable to change with discoveries of new fossils. Current thinking is that the Proterozoic Eon began about 2500 million years ago (usually abbreviated to 'mya') and the Phanerozoic approximately 600 million years ago.

The Phanerozoic Eon is divided into three Eras: *Palaeozoic, Mesozoic* and *Cainozoic,* each characterized by its distinctive plant and animal life. The Palaeozoic (600–248 mya) marks the appearance of most major animal and plant groups, except for a few notables, such as flowering plants and birds. The Mesozoic (248–64 mya), – the time of arrival of many groups that are modern in appearance – was also notable as the time of the great sea reptiles (plesiosaurs and ichthyosaurs), great land reptiles (dinosaurs) and the origin of flowering plants and flying vertebrates (pterosaurs and birds). The Cainozoic (64 mya to the present) saw the dominance of flowering plants, a switch on land from dominant reptiles to mammals and, within the last three million years, the appearance of manlike apes.

Man is a very late inhabitant of the Earth, appearing only within the last 100,000 years, and the enormous history he follows is too vast to really comprehend.

Collecting and studying fossils opens a small window for us through which to glimpse this vast history. The images of long-dead plants and animals that fossils show us are but a vague impression of the true richness and variety of life on Earth.

The History of the Earth	PLANTS	INVERTEBRATES	CRANIATES
Tertiary and Quaternary Mammals took over on land (modern man arrived 100,000 years ago) and birds dominated the air. Insects evolved with flowering plants. In the sea, fishes and whales thrived. 64mya			
Cretaceous Dinosaurs continued to evolve. Pterosaurs and flowering plants appeared. In the sea, echinoids and fishes abounded. 144mya			
Jurassic Dinosaurs dominated the land and the first bird and mammals appeared. Seas swarmed with invertebrates and large reptiles. 213mya			
Triassic Forerunners of the dinosaurs appeared among ginkgos and other plants. Sea urchins and ammonites flourished in the sea. 248mya			
Permian Large reptiles were dominant on land. Giant ferns developed. Cephalopods, bivalves and the last trilobites lived in the sea. 286mya			
Carboniferous Amphibians lived in the vast swamps, and large insects hawked among giant tree ferns. Corals and brachiopods thrived. 360mya			
Devonian Armoured fish lived in rivers, brachiopods and nautiloids filled the seas. Amphibians evolved amid simple plants. 408mya			
Silurian Spore-bearing plants and small, fishlike vertebrates. The sea was filled with invertebrates and the first sharks. 438mya			
Ordovician Marine invertebrates evolved new forms, such as the trilobite, sea snail and cephalopod. Free-floating graptolites appeared. 505mya			
Cambrian Seas teamed with trilobites, brachiopods and molluscs. 'Mystery' animals included the strange *Hallucigenia*. 590mya			
Precambrian First traces of life (2500mya) include stromatolites. Blue-green algae and Ediacara fauna arrived much later. 4600mya			

HOW FOSSILS ARE FORMED

In order to understand how fossils are formed, we need first to examine the natural processes – occurring today, just as much as in the past – that allow fossilization to take place.

The essential requirement for fossilization is burial. An organism has to become buried before the usual processes of nature cause it to be destroyed through scavenging and decay, otherwise its bodily chemicals will return to the surrounding ecosystem leaving no trace of its former existence.

Burial, in turn, requires erosion of rock through the action of rain, wind, heat and cold. Even the largest and most durable of rocks can be split by heating and cooling and, once split, the rock fragments will gradually become worn down to boulders, pebbles and, finally, to sand grains and fine silt. The smallest particles – sands, silts and muds – are called sediments and it is these that are carried by rivers to lakes or the sea, where they are finally deposited in layers on the lake bottom or sea floor. These sediments, which are constantly 'raining' onto the lake or sea floor, will bury anything that may happen to drift there.

Animals and plants living at any time in Earth history may become buried in sediment and stand a chance of becoming fossilized if a set sequence of events occurs. Usually (but not absolutely always, as we shall see), the organism must die – either naturally of old age, or due to disease, predation or a change in living conditions. If the organism already lives in water – or better still on the sea floor – then its chances of being buried are very high. Shellfish, for example, live in the shallow-water sediments of sea shores or estuaries and so are rapidly buried when they die. As a result, there tends to be a bias in the fossil record in favour of sediment-living creatures.

The chances of a land-living animal or plant becoming buried and fossilized are that much smaller. Once it has died, the organism must be buried quite quickly, otherwise it will rot and disappear. In order for it to be buried its remains must usually be washed into a river and carried directly to a lake, or the sea. Here the body should finally sink to the bottom, where it will become slowly buried in sediments. Obviously, the longer burial takes, the greater the opportunity for scavenging and rotting to occur, and the less complete the organism will be when it finally fossilizes.

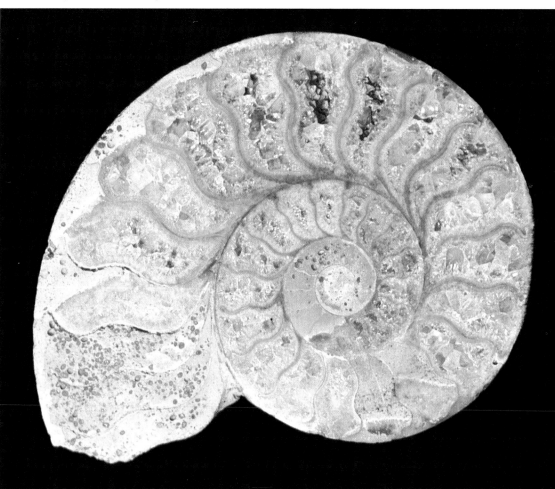

Left: *Silica has crystallized in the once-hollow chambers of this ammonite, leaving the shell itself (the yellow boundary layer) in tact.*

Above right: *The woody tissue of this tree has been largely replaced by opal, but traces of the vascular tissue and growth rings are still visible.*

Right: *Fossilization can occur in a number of ways. After the object is buried, the organic content will rot or be dissolved, leaving a light, fragile fossil (A). Sometimes the spaces left may become filled with minerals, producing a typical petrified bone (B). Or the object may be completely dissolved by acidic ground water, leaving a hollow mould in the rock (C), which may be filled by percolating minerals, leaving a natural cast of the original (D).*

Taphonomy

The whole series of events that may lead to the burial of an organism can vary enormously, and can tell the scientist much about the animal's general environment and the conditions in which it died. This interesting area of detective work has become specialized in its own right and has led to the formation of a branch of palaeontology known as *taphonomy* (meaning, literally, the study of the 'laws of burial'). For this sort of work, the condition of not only the fossil itself, but also the rocks surrounding it are of vital importance to scientific evaluation. It is very important to remember this when collecting fossils in the field. Much crucial information could be lost if, in the general excitement of your discovery, you are too impatient to 'get the fossil out'.

Fossilization

Once burial has begun to occur, the organism no longer risks being disturbed directly. The process of sedimentation continues unceasingly and the sediments thicken above the remains. Rotting continues to occur at this time, and the soft tissues decay, leaving only the harder skeletal parts in most cases. As the sediment layers increase in thickness about the remains they become heavier, and, like a very slow, but remorseless press, the sediment squeezes itself around the trapped organism, sometimes causing the weaker parts to collapse inwards so that it becomes more or less flat. In addition, the sediment itself also compacts (so that all the particles are pushed closer together) and eventually reforms as rock. Such sedimentary rock, as it is called, can vary in consistency from soft clays to very hard sandstones and limestones.

Once trapped in the sedimentary rock, the fate of the organism is sealed: it is destined to become a fossil. Fossils, however, can be of a surprising variety of types. In the simplest condition, the hard skeleton of the organism will be preserved practically unaltered with the passage of time until it is discovered many millions of years later. In many cases, ground water, which percolates through sedimentary rock and frequently contains minerals, may deposit the minerals in the tissue spaces within the skeleton of the organism, so that the skeleton can be said to become mineralized, or petrified (meaning, literally, 'turned to stone'). Sometimes skeletal minerals may actually be replaced by these percolating minerals, so that no trace of the original skeleton is preserved but a perfect replica is produced in stone; a case of complete petrification. If the ground water is acidic, this may actually dissolve the original skeleton, leaving hollow moulds in the rocks. Lovely examples of this type of fossil have been found in Scotland (Elgin) and Australia. Such rocky moulds can be filled with latex rubber or natural minerals, such as opal, to form perfect casts of the original skeletons.

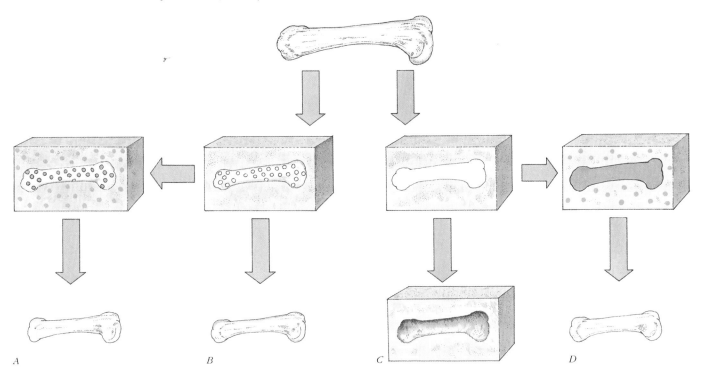

A   B   C   D

11

Plants: carbon copies

Plant remains frequently undergo a process known as distillation. The enormous weight of sediment in which they are buried drives off the lighter elements (oxygen, nitrogen and hydrogen) leaving a residue of carbon. This process can produce beautifully preserved leaves and fruiting bodies in the form of a thin carbon film. At a more extreme level, coal seams are the distilled remains of huge forests of trees buried and compressed under river sediments.

Peat is a partly distilled form of fossil plant remains and is also a good preservative. Many ancient bones have been found in peat bogs, and pollen grains are also well preserved in peat. The latter can tell scientists a great deal about vegetation of the past, which in turn can inform us about the climatic conditions. However, peat is relatively young in geological terms, dating back tens of thousands rather than millions of years, and the remains contained within peat bogs are usually referred to as 'sub-fossil', meaning that they are not quite old enough to be considered as true fossils. They are remains that would form true fossils if left buried for a few more million years.

Other exceptional fossils have been found in amber, the sap of coniferous trees, which is very sticky and frequently traps small insects and, more rarely, small vertebrates (such as small tree lizards and frogs) in beautiful condition. Much amber of Cainozoic age has been found on the shores of the Baltic Sea and provides important information about delicate animals that would be too fragile to preserve as normal fossils.

Finally, there are two types of sediment that may form on land: volcanic ash and sand. Volcanic ash is usually too corrosive to preserve the remains of living creatures, though some remarkable tracks of animals and early Man have been recovered in East Africa (see page 15). Just occasionally, organisms may be preserved by being engulfed in wind-blown sand among dunes or in dust storms. In these conditions, animals, in particular, frequently become dried and 'mummified'. A few dinosaurs have been preserved in this way and the sands that surrounded such a dried carcass have preserved an impression of the dried skin of the creature in fine detail.

Trace fossils

Some trace fossils, such as eggs, are preserved in much the same way as skeletal fossils, and in rare instances may even preserve the remains of developing young inside. Other trace fossils, such as footprints, require slightly different conditions. In this case, the prints must be left on a soft surface, such as a drying river bed, or the shore line of a lake or moist river bank. The prints then need to dry, at least partly, before they are

Left: *The organic remains of this plant are shown as a beautifully clear carbonized imprint on a layer of grey siltstone. Compressed carbon residues preserve particularly good evidence of the form of plant leaves.*

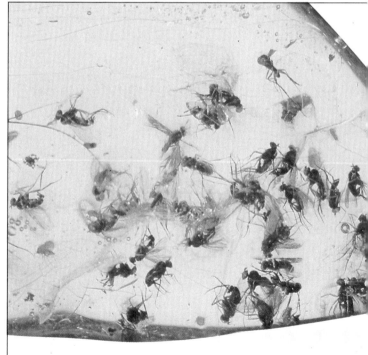

covered by fresh sediment of a slightly different kind. The difference in sediment types between the layer on which the print was left and the covering layer provides an *interface* (or layer of separation), which will eventually reveal the print once the sediment has hardened into rock and is split, by weathering or a geologist's hammer.

Unfortunately, it is frequently impossible to be sure of the sort of organism that left such traces and so palaeontologists have devised a different way of classifying these puzzling remains. Trace fossils can be divided into the following categories:

Immobility traces: resting places.

Feeding traces: passages or tunnels in leaves, grazing traces, tooth or claw marks, borings into hard substrates.

Locomotion traces: crawling, running, walking, swimming, flying traces.

Traces of metabolism: excrement, traces of illness (parasitism, death throes, limb repairs, callouses, hard tissue disorders).

Traces of reproduction: eggs, nests, egg shell fragments.

Trace fossils can often tell us a great deal about the environment in which the traces were left, and so reveal a surprising amount about the conditions of life at the time and the organism that left the traces.

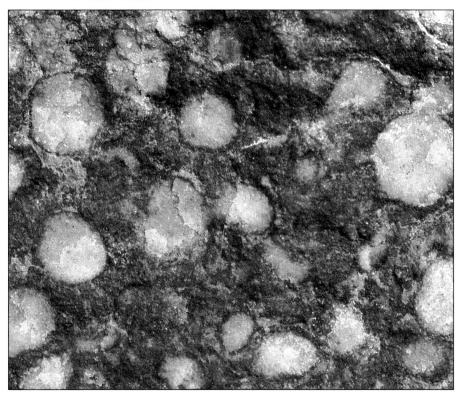

Left: *Amber, used to make jewellery, can also be a source of fossils. This sticky sap from conifer trees occasionally contains small organisms, such as these beautifully preserved insects.*

Above right: *This rock was a beach sand in Cambrian times. The circular structures are the ends of pipes of quartz that have filled ancient worm burrows.*

Right: *Footprints, such as these of a small (two-metre-long) carnivorous dinosaur, are comparatively rare finds, but when they are discovered, it is not unusual to find large numbers in an area.*

LOOKING FOR FOSSILS

Only a very small percentage of plants and animals living at any one time ever become fossilized but despite this, some rocks are known to contain vast numbers of fossils and these can be found quite easily if you know how and where to look for them.

Which rocks?

Rocks that started as molten material which cooled and solidified, such as granites and lavas, are unlikely to yield fossils. It would be expected that any organisms engulfed by such rock would have been destroyed beyond recognition. Of course, as with almost any rule that we can make up, there are examples that contradict it. Pompeii, whose inhabitants were engulfed by the volcanic ash spewed out by Mount Vesuvius nearly 2000 years ago, shows in horrific detail the natural moulds of thousands of people and their domestic animals. These remains are, however, a part of human cultural history and are therefore studied by archaeologists, rather than palaeontologists, and so do not really qualify as fossils in the generally accepted sense. A better example would perhaps be the remarkable discoveries made by Mary Leakey of 3.6 million-year-old footprints of the fossil ancestors of Man and contemporary animals in East Africa (Laetoli). These remarkable footprints were left on a layer of ash that had recently settled on the ground following a violent volcanic eruption in the area. Such circumstances are extremely rare, and their discovery even rarer. The really exceptional nature of both of these examples just emphasizes the general truth of the statement above.

The really important rocks, as far as searching for fossils is concerned, are *sedimentary* rocks (see page 11), ie. clays, shales, limestones and some of the finer sandstones. (Coarser sandstones tend to be too porous and any fossils contained therein are often dissolved away, and they often do not form such a clear impression.)

Where to find fossil-bearing rocks

The best places to find such rocks vary enormously from place to place, but in general are simply anywhere that rock has been exposed beneath the soil. Obvious examples are eroding cliffs on the sea shore, railway or road cuttings, building sites (occasionally), abandoned and working quarries, and river banks. In less heavily urbanized parts of the world, large areas of the countryside may be undeveloped 'outback', semi-arid desert, or desert where there is little vegetation cover and a lot of exposed rock, which may be weathered away quite quickly. Such areas are frequently very rich in fossils.

There are two main ways to find fossiliferous rocks. You may be lucky and happen upon some fossils during an outing in the country, or hear from a friend of a particular place where fossils have been found. Alternatively, you can use a geological map. Such maps are very detailed surveys of the types of rock, and their ages, to be found in different areas. They are available today for almost all areas of the globe, and allow would-be fossil hunters to pin-point certain areas to visit. Your choices will depend upon where you live, how far you are prepared to travel, the particular fossils you want to collect, and the age of rocks in which you are especially interested.

You may be able to enlist some on-the-spot help with finding fossils by contacting local museums, or geological clubs or societies, which are actively interested in their own geological 'patches'.

Fossil-collecting equipment

The right field equipment is essential for anyone intending to look for and collect fossils. The type of equipment you will need will vary depending on what sort of fossils you are looking for and where.

Firstly you will need to think about appropriate personal clothing and protective wear. Many fossil sites are both exposed and remote, so safety is a prime consideration. Strong, waterproof walking boots are essential for scrabbling over loose rock and protecting the feet from being crushed

Right: *There are a wide variety of different places in which you can hope to find fossils; generally, anywhere that rock has been exposed beneath the soil is a potential site. Building sites and railway and road cuttings can all be good sources, but these busy places can be dangerous for the untrained, and you may find, in any case, that safety regulations make it impossible for you to look for fossils at some such sites.*

Instead, try visiting your nearest coastline. Coastal areas are perhaps the most popular sites for fossil collectors; the sea, wind and rain do an excellent job here in exposing fresh rock, and, if the right rocks are exposed, rich fossil pickings may be available. Indeed, in some places, if the fossils are not collected they are likely to be destroyed by erosion.

under boulders. A helmet, such as workmen wear on building sites, is also essential for protection from falling rocks on cliff faces and in case you accidentally slip over on rocky terrain. General clothes should be hard-wearing and comfortable (you may be surprised at some of the positions you will need to adopt to be able to dig for fossils!). A strong pair of gloves for heavy hammering and chiselling and protective goggles to stop sharp and hot splinters of stone entering the eyes and causing severe injury or blindness are also essential protective wear.

For actually excavating fossils you will need a hammer (preferably two, of different weights), some cold chisels, a small trowel, various brushes, and a pot or several tubes of glue. You will also need small cloth or plastic bags, paper or plastic strips, a waterproof marker pen or wax crayon, a notebook, and, ideally, a camera.

Right: *You are unlikely to find anything quite as impressive as these footprints of early Man, unearthed by the palaeontologist Mary Leakey in 1978. This remarkable set of footprints was found preserved in a layer of hardened volcanic ash in East Africa. The tracks date back 3.6 million years and proved conclusively that early manlike creatures walked in a completely upright fashion.*

Dealing with discoveries

There is an immense thrill associated with finding fossils. Looking at and holding the remains of an organism that may have last seen the light of day 200 million years or more ago is quite a humbling experience. Today more people are finding more time for leisure activities, and among these a proportion are discovering the joy of fossil collecting as a hobby. Equally, there is now a thriving market for fossils – which can change hands for substantial amounts of money – and this is encouraging an increasing number of commercial collectors (who make a living out of collecting and selling fossils). In the long term, this sort of increased 'pressure' on geological sites may cause them to become effectively worked out, and therefore very difficult to find fossils at. Bear this in mind, then, and remember that, as discussed on page 8, fossils are part of our national heritage.

When you discover a fossil, you should do a number of things before removing it from the geological strata in which you found it. For the information it contains to be useful in the future to palaeontologists and geologists alike, you should make a careful note of the position in which you found it in the rock. (Careful notes of the place where the fossil was found, and a diagram of its position in the rock are essential, and, ideally, you should take a photograph of the fossil in position.) Such notes are of vital importance for any future research on the fossil.

Take great care when removing fossils to ensure that they are not broken. It must be stressed that the fossils you see in a museum have been cleaned purely for display purposes. Specimens found on site should not be scrupulously cleaned before they are placed in the specimen bag. It is far better to remove the fossil in a small bed of sediment if this is at all possible. This will protect the specimen from damage during transportation and will also keep in association any potentially crucial geological information about the circumstances in which the fossil became buried (its taphonomy). It may also make the location easier to trace on a future visit. Wrap the fossil in soft cloth, paper, or a plastic bag, and slip in with it some notes on where you found the specimen. It is surprising how easily this is forgotten if several specimens are collected during the course of a single day's work.

Excavating large fossils

Large specimens need very careful handling and this is a skilled job that is best left to a team of museum staff or trained palaeontological fieldworkers. (It is clearly impossible for one person to simply lift a large fossil – which may weigh several tonnes in the case of a dinosaur fossil – and put it in his or her collecting bag!) These professionals will have experience in excavating and labelling fossils so that they can be accurately reassembled in the laboratory.

Firstly, the whole of the area where the skeleton lies needs to be very carefully cleared, roughly down to the level of all exposed bone. When this has been done, all digging stops for several days while the area is carefully mapped out and photographed. Plans are drawn and a detailed record is made of each bone and its position. When this tedious, but very important task is completed, the area around the perimeter of the fossil is dug out to form a wide trench. The rock beneath the skeleton is then excavated, leaving a protective and strengthening thickness of sediment below the bone layer.

When a manageable area of the skeleton has been undermined, the upper surface is coated with wet paper, which acts as a separating layer, and this in turn is covered by layers of scrim, or cut strips of hemp sacking soaked in plaster-of-Paris. The plaster bandages are wound around both upper and lower surfaces of the fossil and left to harden. The protected block can then be labelled (in preparation for reassembly back in the laboratory of the museum). Once carefully pulled away from the remainder of the skeleton, the free edges are papered and plastered, and the specimen is then moved, in comparative safety, to waiting transport.

Polyurethane foam jackets have sometimes been used on site to protect large specimens. These have the advantage of being both light and strong, but are used relatively rarely at present because of the difficulty of transporting the chemicals necessary to make the foam, and the problems caused by toxic gases, which the chemicals give off when mixed.

In the laboratory all the careful note-taking pays off. The labelled blocks can be reassembled accurately, and the lengthy process of cleaning, scientific study (where all the notes become vitally important to interpretation of the skeleton) and the conservation of the material begins, perhaps in preparation to make the specimen into a museum exhibit.

Below left: *Major fossil excavations, such as this one for the remains of fossil Man at Koobi Fora near Lake Turkana in Kenya, need to be undertaken with enormous care and precision, not only to prevent damage to the fossils, but also to ensure that every scrap of evidence is obtained.*

Below: *Half way through the excavation of a large ichthyosaur skeleton in the outback of Australia the skeleton is supported on a bed of rock. When a manageable block has been undermined, it will be carefully plastered, labelled and removed.*

Below: *The paddle of the ichthyosaur is protected with layers of plaster-soaked strips of sacking. When the bone is pulled away from the rest of the skeleton, the exposed surface will be treated in the same way.*

Right: *Large fossils can be very difficult to move. Here a block and tackle is being used to lift a heavy slab of rock with a dinosaur bone in it from the rock face at Dinosaur National Monument in Utah.*

THE THEORY OF EVOLUTION

T he theory of *evolution* – the theory that organisms have the potential to change their physical appearance and genetic make-up with the passage of time – underpins all the work of modern palaeontologists. A brief overview of this subject will show that palaeontology – the study of fossils – is one of several crucially important areas of research that bear directly on our modern understanding of evolution. Indeed in recent years the study of fossils has led to much debate on this very subject.

Evolution has its origins in the activities of natural philosophers of the 17th and 18th centuries, who set themselves the task of cataloguing and then classifying all living organisms in the known world. Their aims were firstly to provide a basis for knowledge of all types of life and, secondly, to arrange the living world into some form of order or hierarchy. They believed that the world had been created in a single divine act and their quest was to try and understand the mind of the Creator of our world.

One of the most successful of these early systematists (as these philosophers who were looking for patterns in nature are called) was Linnaeus, who, in the middle of the 18th century, compiled an extensive list of species or organisms. These species were given names and clustered together into related sets or groups. The fact that it was often possible to group together animals and plants that looked similar (for example, catlike creatures, ranging from domestic cats to lions, or cone-bearing trees) implied

The Evolution of the Horse

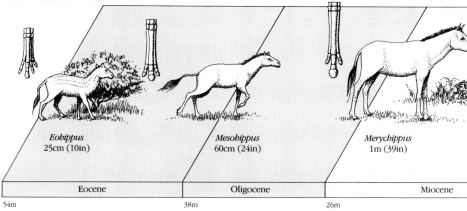

Eohippus
25cm (10in)

Mesohippus
60cm (24in)

Merychippus
1m (39in)

| Eocene | Oligocene | Miocene |

54m   38m   26m

some form or order in Nature, which seemed to indicate the way in which the Creator's mind worked. This view of the order in the world and Creation was challenged on several occasions around these times, but to little avail.

The first half of the 19th century saw the rise in importance of the work of palaeontologists. Around the turn of the century a most important breakthrough occurred when the anatomist and palaeontologist Cuvier, in Paris, was able to show that animals had become extinct. (Up until that time it was assumed that God would not have wasted time creating animals that would become extinct.) Cuvier also noticed that extinct animals looked different to living ones, even though they seemed to be quite similar in most respects (for example, they may have been larger or smaller than, or slightly different in shape from, living ones).

The whole intellectual climate was changing and was, in effect, preparing itself for the publication of the work of Charles Darwin in 1859. Darwin's book, *On the Origin of Species*, summarized much work that Darwin had done since the 1830s on the question of why organisms fall into related groups, why organisms became extinct, and why fossil organisms look different to living ones. The answer he devised was one that relied on a process he could see occuring in Nature, which he named 'Natural Selection'.

Below: *Three important scientists who helped develop modern views about evolution. From left to right: Carl Linnaeus, Georges Cuvier and Charles Darwin.*

Right: *Painstaking work is carried out by palaeontologists in the laboratory. Here the hard rocky matrix is being removed from the delicate skull of a dinosaur.*

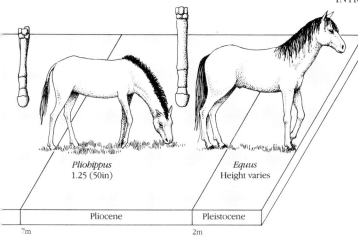

Pliohippus
1.25 (50in)

Equus
Height varies

| Pliocene | Pleistocene |

7m   2m

Left: *This simplified diagram demonstrates the evolutionary process. Time is shown in millions of years and geological epochs along the base. The earliest horselike creatures were small, had four toes and were browsers. In time horses became larger and their toes reduced to a single hoof. These changes left them better able to live on open grassy plains.*

the pest insects. A few 'lucky' insects had some special feature that gave them resistance to the pesticide. As time went on, only the resistant insects survived and bred young, which inherited the resistance. Eventually these became dominant within the population and the pesticide ceased to be effective. The insect could be said to have 'evolved' pesticide resistance. This is clearly a rather unnatural example, but hopefully explains the principle Darwin was trying to establish. It is survival of the 'best' individuals that tends to drive evolution in the natural world.

The importance of palaeontology to this scheme is that by studying fossils, it may be possible to see evolution occuring. The sorts of changes that may have been responsible for transforming one species into another, or into a completely different type of organism, would require long periods of time. The geological timescale provides immense periods of time and perhaps the opportunity to catch evolution 'in the act'.

The birth of life itself is one of the most vexed of all questions in modern palaeontology, and to find answers to the questions posed it has been necessary to involve a whole range of sciences, including biology, molecular biology, astronomy, physics and chemistry. Here, we briefly examine this problem by looking at the conditions on the primitive Earth, and then at those things that are necessary in order to establish life.

The primitive Earth

The oldest rocks date back 3750 million years, and even these show some evidence of erosion, which indicates that there was some sort of environment on Earth even at this time. Astronomers suggest that the Earth probably condensed from a cloud of interstellar dust and gas and was drawn together by enormous gravitational forces to form a tremendously hot, molten planet around 4600 million years ago, as our solar system formed. As the planet cooled, Earth became very volcanically active, creating huge volumes of toxic gases – hydrogen, nitrogen, carbon monoxide, carbon dioxide, hydrogen sulphide and sulphur dioxide – and water vapour. These elements would have formed the early atmosphere. No oxygen was to be found in this early atmosphere, and indeed no clear traces of oxygen can be found in the chemical structure of the rocks until about 2000 million years ago. From then on, the atmosphere gradually came to resemble the air that we breathe today.

He noted that all organisms tend to vary – no two individuals are exactly the same (unless they are identical twins, of course) – and that if conditions become difficult for life, only those best suited to surviving those conditions will prosper. If these conditions continue for long enough, then only those individuals with the favourable characters will breed and pass on their attributes to the next generation. Given long enough, then, the character of a whole species could be subtly altered by such changes in conditions. That

is to say, the species would *evolve* to suit the changing conditions.

An extreme example of this sort of process can be seen today with the use of pesticides. Many insects feed on and damage crops and farmers use a pesticide to kill these insects and improve the harvest. However, after a while the pesticide becomes less effective, the insects become more abundant, and a new pesticide becomes necessary. What has happened is that the original pesticide killed most, but not all, of

EARLY LIFE ON EARTH

Despite the rather hostile nature of the early atmosphere of the Earth, the simple gases seem to have been sufficient to allow for the formation of the earliest biological molecules – the first step on the road to the appearance of life. Most of the gases are able to react together provided they can be given enough energy of the right sort to start their reactions. The Sun was the source of most energy, especially short-wave energy (which is today shielded out by the ozone layer). There would also have been considerable heat energy from radioactive rocks and from volcanoes. Lightning and meteorite impacts would also have been of considerable importance in generating energy to promote these necessary chemical reactions in the atmosphere.

A measure of proof of this scenario comes from work started by Stanley Miller in Chicago in 1953. By firing electrical discharges through experimental apparatus containing the toxic gases (listed on page 19) for long periods of time, Miller was able to create a wide range of important biological molecules, including fatty acids, sugars and parts of the building blocks of DNA and RNA. It therefore seems likely from what we can deduce about the early atmosphere of the primitive Earth, and from the work of chemists today, that the Earth would have quite rapidly built up a surprisingly complex 'chemical soup' in its oceans. The next major obstacle to our understanding is how these interesting molecules could have come together to form something that we could call a living organism. Living organisms have a number of properties that are lacking in a 'chemical soup'. Most important of these are their ability to grow (in other words, to take in and use energy) and to reproduce (to make new individuals).

Models for early organisms

There are currently a number of ideas as to how this might have taken place, none of which is proven or agreed upon. All tend to rely on something causing the 'chemical soup' to become more concentrated over time. It could be that in some areas the water was confined in shallow lakes or small pools, which gradually, through evaporation, became more concentrated. Such circumstances would cause the molecules to begin to behave somewhat differently, separating out into groups and forming small spherical droplets (known as coacervates or microspheres). These small spheres have a membrane around them, which allows chemical reactions to happen on their surface.

Unfortunately, interesting structures though they are, these small spheres with chemicals attached are a long way from true early cells. What has to develop is a membrane that can control what passes into the cell and the chemical reactions to harness energy for growth, and the chemical machinery to allow for reproduction. As yet we do not know how this occurred.

Proterozoic fossils: the earliest evidence of life

The earliest forms of life on Earth would have lived in an atmosphere that was devoid of oxygen, completely unlike the atmosphere today. Although many people tend to assume that oxygen is essential for life, there are, in fact, bacteria living today that can survive with a complete absence of oxygen (indeed some can be killed by oxygen), especially in the black muds in estuaries. These 'sulphur bacteria', as they are known, almost certainly existed on primitive Earth.

The very earliest organisms for which we have fossil evidence, however, did not live under the mud, but above it, in large, mushroom-shaped colonies, and are known as *stromatolites* (meaning, literally, 'matted stones'). They are curiously shaped mats or clumps of rock, which, when cut through and polished, show a very finely layered structure not unlike the surface of a freshly cut cabbage. Quite what these structures were remained a mystery until some living examples were discovered. Living stromatolites are today found around the Indian and Pacific Oceans in areas where the water is particularly salty.

Stromatolites are the only widespread and obvious form of life for the first 2000 million years of the Proterozoic. The oldest known stromatolitic structures have been identified in rocks that date from between 3400 and 3500 mya, according to present estimates, and come from Warrawoona in Western Australia.

According to recent research on this material, these fossils were benthic (lived on the sea-floor) in relatively shallow water and may well have been exposed on occasion both to the atmosphere and to intense ultraviolet radiation from the sun. (Remember that at this time in Earth's history the atmosphere had not yet become enriched with oxygen and there was no shielding ozone layer to filter out many of the sun's harmful rays.) From their earliest appearance through to the Late Proterozoic Eon (about 600 mya), stromatolites became increasingly abundant and varied. After this, however, these forms of life declined in abundance.

Left: *Stromatolites are often seen most clearly when they are cut in sections and polished, as here. The outline of the domed top is visible at the top of the picture, beneath this are the fine layers of sediment that were trapped by the mucous secretions of blue-green algae.*

Right: *In some parts of Australasia (this picture was taken at Shark Bay in Australia) large colonies of living stromatolites are still found. They tend to survive only in very salty conditions that exclude predators such as echinoderms and snails.*

Living stromatolites

The living examples of stromatolites probably give us some insight into the harsh conditions that prevailed on earth throughout the Proterozoic. For example, those seen in Shark Bay in Eastern Australia consist of thin, jelly-covered, matlike colonies of blue-green algae. Blue-green algae are not 'algae' in the sense of seaweed or the green slime in freshwater ponds, but, rather, are photosynthetic or plantlike bacteria. These remarkable organisms can harness the energy of sunlight in order to convert simple chemicals into more complex biological molecules for growth and reproduction. Furthermore, experiments with living examples show that they have remarkable powers of survival. Blue-greens are able to resist the damage to their DNA that ultraviolet light can cause because they have special DNA repair molecules, as well as the blue-green pigment, which acts as a shield to filter out the worst of this radiant energy. It is also a fact that the sticky, jelly-like covering that these microbes secrete around themselves catches fine sand and mud grains, which form a further protective layer. The layers of mud that stick to the surface of colonies of blue-greens account for the layered appearance of the fossil stromatolites.

The fact that stromatolites survive today only in very inhospitable places, such as hot briny pools, may well indicate the reason for their eventual decline in the Late Proterozoic. Today these conditions exclude predators, such as echinoderms and snails, which would otherwise feed upon blue-green colonies. It may well have been the appearance of larger and more complex predatory animals in the Late Proterozoic that fed upon the blue-green reefs that led to their marked decline in abundance and variety.

FROM WATER TO LAND

The activities of these photosynthetic blue-green algae in the primitive oceans led to a gradual rise in the levels of oxygen in the atmosphere so that by about 1500 million years ago, the air was much more like that which we breathe today. The rise in levels of oxygen had a number of consequences for life. Firstly it provided a protective layer around the planet because it allowed the ozone layer to develop. (The ozone layer is responsible for filtering out many of the Sun's harmful rays – the very things that allowed life to start in the first place!) Oxygen also enabled development of much more energetic forms of life, and thus spurred the process of evolution.

In the latter part of the Proterozoic Eon, blue-green algae became less abundant and gave way to other types of photosynthetic organisms, which were not bacteria but more closely related to true plants; these were the true algae. These sorts of plants were again very simple forms of life in that they tended to be single-celled, but they were larger than the photosynthetic bacteria (the blue-greens) and had a discrete nucleus to each cell and photosynthetic pigment held in small capsules within the cytoplasm.

Modern true algae are separated and classified into a number of groups on the basis of their pigments (the coloured chemicals they contain, which allow them to use the energy of sunlight). The chief groups are yellow algae, red algae, brown algae and green algae. Each group has a very distinctive type of pigment and biochemistry, and it is supposed that such fundamental differences, which have been maintained through to the present day, must have arisen during the Proterozoic Eon.

Early true algae

Naturally, the fossil record of algae is not very rich; for the most part these organisms tend to have soft tissues, which preserve very poorly. However, some very early algae seem to be identifiable in chert deposits in the Bitter Springs Formation of Australia. (Chert is glasslike rock, which derives from a jellylike substance composed of silica. This accumulated on the floor of ancient oceans and trapped organisms, such as algae, before finally hardening.) These rocks date back about 1000 million years, and found within them are traces not only of blue-green algae, but also of larger forms with nuclei within the cells, which must have been early true

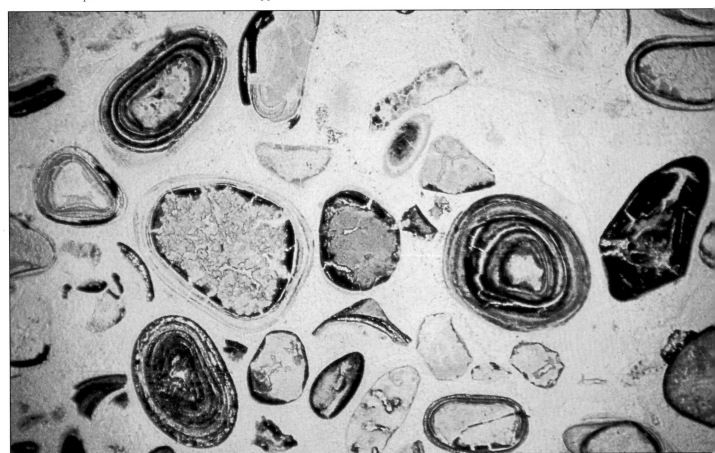

algae. It is not certain when the first true algae appeared on Earth, but these findings would suggest that it was at least 1000 million years ago.

Apart from the cherts, which give us an unusual insight into the variety of microscopic plant life during the Proterozoic, the majority of our knowledge of the early plants of this time, and into the early part of the Phanerozoic Eon, comes from the algae whose soft tissues were supported by skeletons of silica or lime.

These calcareous (calcium carbonate) algae were prodigious reef or rock builders of their times. They built up layers of rock with their own skeletons, or trapped and bound limestone particles drifting in the water. Calcareous algae included representatives of the red and green true algae, as well as stromatolitic blue-greens. Somewhere within the early true algae – and more particularly the green algae – were the ancestors of the early land plants.

Right: *Stromatolitic remains from the Pre-Cambrian are widely found. Thin sections of chert frequently reveal the remains of blue-green algae.*

Below left: *This thin section of chert shows the fossil remains of some of the earliest forms of life, about 2000 million years old. All are varieties of blue-green algae.*

Below: *This shoreline shows the develoment of true algae. Algae of this type must have begun to occur on Earth about 1000mya.*

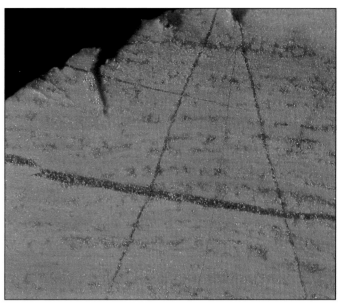

EARLY LAND PLANTS

One of the most striking features of present-day landscapes is the green vegetation: shrubs, broad-leaved trees, grasses, ferns, conifers and so on. These are all known as vascular plants because they possess a system of water-carrying tubes (the vascular system), which are supported by special strengthening materials and give the skeleton necessary support on land. The first evidence of these organisms is to be found in rocks of the Silurian Period (over 400 million years old), and it must be assumed that the surface of the land prior to this time was bare, or at best covered in places with a thin scumlike layer of algae, such as you may notice on the trunks of modern trees.

The earliest fossil vascular plants are *Cooksonia*, of which several species are known from the Silurian and Devonian Periods in North America, Europe and Asia, and *Rhynia*, from the Silurian Rhynie chert of Scotland. These plants had no roots, leaves or flowers and were really just a cluster of upright forking stems. Most of the stems seem to have ended in a small disc-shaped cap, which contained spores.

The spores, a simple form of seed, pre-sumably drifted away on currents of air. Wind dispersal, such as this, ensured a wide distribution for these early plants, and this is reflected in the wide geographical spread of their fossil record. The lack of a well-developed root system for obtaining water suggests that these types of plant lived only in moist areas, such as lowland marshes, the margins of lakes, and river flood plains.

A second type of vascular plant, which appeared a little later than *Cooksonia*, has been called *Zosterophyllum*. It was very similar to *Cooksonia* in that it had smooth branching stems, but along the sides of its stems were rows of small bag-shaped spor-angia (spore capsules).

These early land plants were literally 'breaking new ground'; there was nothing else to compete with, so they were comple-tely free to colonize any land areas and, as a consequence, they very rapidly spread and diversified. By the early Devonian Period, quite a few different plants are known to have existed, mostly variants of the ones seen above. Some had spiky stems, others tended to be highly branched, which gave them the appearance of small bushes. None of these plants exist today, but a few of those that first appeared in the early Devonian have living relatives. Principal among these are the clubmosses.

Clubmosses

Modern clubmosses, distant relatives of the ferns, are small and live in damp, moun-tainous areas in the UK. Their stems, which tend to divide into pairs (like those of the plants just described), bear a spiral arrangement of small, scaly leaves. The spor-es are borne on the sides of the stems, usually near to the top of the plant. Club-mosses have true roots.

Some clubmosses of the Devonian Period, such as *Drepanophycus*, look very similar to living ones, though many tended to grow to a much larger size. A variety of plants appeared during the Devonian Period, and grew increasingly large in the competition for light and space around the water's edge. This trend put many physical constraints on these early plants. Their weight became an increasing problem, and this led to the development of great masses of strengthen-ing material in the stems and trunks and, eventually, to the formation of the first trees. Some of the most impressive of these were the gigantic clubmoss trees, which grew to a height of 165ft (50m).

Evolution of the seed

Another major innovation brought on by clubmosses was the development of the seed. Large seeds have been found in the

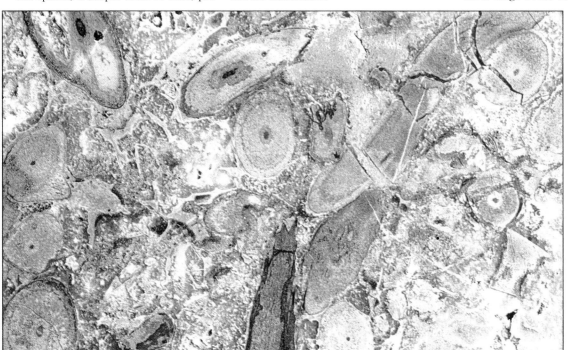

Left: *This section through Rhynie Chert shows the cut stems of the early land plant* Rhynia *(the circular or elliptical shapes). The cross-sections of the stems show the water-carrying tubes essential for a land-living plant.*

Right: Drepanophycus. *A reconstruction of an early clubmoss typical of those of the Devonian Period.*

Far right: *This modern clubmoss,* Lycopodium *from the Central Alps, shows clearly how little these types of plant have changed over the last 380 million years.*

Late Devonian in the USA, and although there is still uncertainty as to what plant produced them, the evolutionary stages of the seed can be traced through clubmosses.

Most clubmosses, like their relatives the ferns, reproduce by scattering identical tiny spores. The exception, *Selaginella*, represents an important stage in the development of a spore into a proper seed. This living clubmoss produces two kinds of spore, one large, the other small. The larger spore acts as the female, and the smaller spore releases mobile male spores, which swim to the female and cause an egg (fertile seed) to be produced. In some cases the fertilized spore remains attached to the parent plant for its early life before falling to the ground, where it will to grow independently.

The fertilized spore can be protected for a while as it begins to grow and some of the giant lycopod trees of the Devonian and Carboniferous Periods show evidence of the retained spores on their branches. True seed-bearing plants use broadly the same sort of arrangement, with a large female seed held on the plant, and much smaller pollen grains that travel (by wind or insects) to the female seed. Differences occur in the various protective and nourishing layers for the seed's growth, but the general principle remains the same.

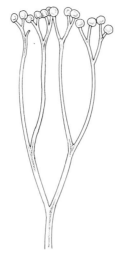

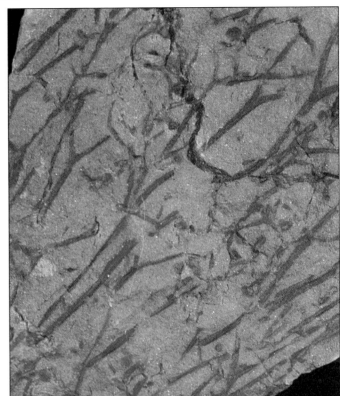

Above: Cooksonia, *another early plant, had a simple stem (with no leaves or scales) ending in small spherical spore cases.*

Right: *This slab of sandstone shows a group of preserved stems of* Cooksonia.

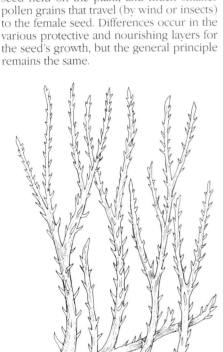

FIRST FORESTS

Some of the most familiar of all plants from the fossil record are those from rocks of the Carboniferous Period because these form the coal deposits that have been mined for centuries. It seems that about 300 million years ago the northern continents (North America, Europe and Asia) were covered by huge, shallow swamps, where the very hot and wet climate encouraged growth of huge forests. In time plants died and fell into the swamp water, and their remains, many of which did not rot, built up thick layers of peat. Judged from the layering of the deposits in the Carboniferous swamps, these forests were from time to time flooded by the sea. The salt water killed off much of the forest vegetation and deposited layers of sand and mud upon the layers of peat. Later the sea would retreat, leaving the land to become recolonized by plants and the forests to return. This cyclical pattern was repeated numerous times over the millions of years of the Late Carboniferous Period and, with the passage of time, the layers of peat were compressed and distilled, first into lignite or brown coal and,

eventually, into coal, and the intervening layers into sandstone and mudstone.

During the period of compression, which led to distillation, the structures of individual plants were more often than not destroyed, though it is frequently possible to make out the impression of leaves on pieces of household coal (even though it has been sent through mechanical crushers). Curiously, the best plant fossils are not found in the coal itself, but in the soft sandstone layers sandwiched between the coal seams. The Carboniferous swamp forests contained a wide variety of plant life ranging from small herbs to shrubs and gigantic trees.

Lycopods (giant clubmosses)

The best known and most remarkable trees of these forests were the giant clubmosses, such as *Lepidodendron*, some of which grew to a height of 100ft(30m), with trunks up to six and a half feet (two metres) thick at the base. Some very good examples of tree trunks of *Lepidodendron* are found at Wadsley in Sheffield, and at the Fossil Forest, Victoria Park, Glasgow. This tree had a broad, but shallowly rooted base, the branching roots extending out horizontally along the ground surface. The roots are

covered in small oval scars left where small rootlets have broken off. The trunk was long and straight and covered with leaf scars, which form a very pleasing mozaic effect. The timber of this tree would not have been of very good quality as it had less hard tissue than modern trees. The upper branches of the tree branched regularly and ended in clusters of long strap-shaped leaves, interspersed with podlike, spore-bearing cones.

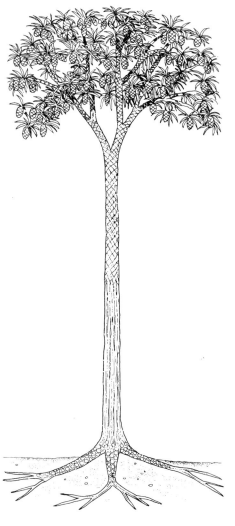

Left: *This close-up of the trunk of the tree-sized clubmoss* Lepidodendron *shows the very distinctive leaf scars of this plant.*

Above: *The clubmoss* Lepidodendron *had large podlike spore-bearing cones on its upper branches and branched roots.*

Sphenopsids (Horsetails)

This group also produced large treelike forms in the Carboniferous. Today this group is represented by mostly small forms that live in wet areas. The largest British species grows to about six and a half feet (2m) high, but some species from the tropics can grow as high as 36ft(11m) because they scramble over other vegetation to support themselves. The stems of these plants are distinctively jointed, and from each joint arises a ring of slender branches with small scalelike leaves. They produce cone-shaped spore capsules on the tip of the stem, but they also spread by an underground root, which sends up new shoots as it spreads through the ground. The best example of a Carboniferous treelike version of these plants was *Calamites*, a large, thick-stemmed plant that grew to a height of 15ft(18m) or more. *Sphenophyllum*, another common horsetail found in the Carboniferous forests, was a successful herbaceous plant and more like smaller living forms.

Below: *The gymnosperm tree* Neuropteris *grew very abundantly during the Carboniferous Period. The foliage of this plant is particularly well preserved here.*

Right and far right: *The treelike horsetail* Calamites *grew from an underground root (or rhizome). The fossilized stem of the plant is shown in the photograph.*

Gymnosperms

Two groups of Gymnosperms produced tree types in the Carboniferous: the seed-ferns and the cordaitales. The seed-ferns are mostly plants with slender woody stems and very fernlike leaves (hence their rather confusing name – they are not, in fact, ferns at all). Their key feature is found on their leaves, which do not have spore holders but small pouches containing pollen or small seeds (*Emplectopteris*). Cordaitales are represented in the Carboniferous by very large trees, which grew up to 100ft(30m) tall. These trees were probably less dependent upon water for their reproduction than were seedferns, as they were able to release airborne pollen, and, as a result, were probably associated with upland areas away from the swamps. These trees had heavier wooden trunks and in many ways resembled conifers, although their leaves were broader.

The herb and shrub layers of the Carboniferous forests were occupied by seedferns of a bewildering variety, along with some true ferns, clubmosses, and small horsetails.

MESOZOIC PLANT LIFE

The settled warm and wet climatic conditions that led to the profusion of plant life in the Devonian and Carboniferous Periods were disrupted during the following Permian Period (the last Period of the Palaeozoic Era. This change in climate ushered in a different pattern of vegetation types, which became established during the middle part of the Phanerozoic Eon: the Mesozoic Era. Many species that were adapted to warmer and continuously moist conditions became extinct and were replaced by hardier types.

Another factor that may also have had a significant effect on the survival of certain plant groups was the appearance of browsing vertebrates. In the Permian and Triassic Periods, large numbers of moderate-sized – 3–13ft(1–4m)-long – vertebrates (synapsids in particular, see page 57) appeared for the first time in Earth history. These low browsers would undoubtedly have had an impact on the plants living at the time, and may account for the rise in tough leaves and seeds to counteract these predators.

In the latter part of the Triassic and during the Jurassic Period, the synapsids were succeeded by some of the largest plant-eaters that have ever roamed the Earth: the sauropod dinosaurs of up to 100ft(30m) in length. These latter types were also the first high browsers to appear and used their long necks, which could reach 40ft(12m) high or more, to prey upon the tall conifer trees. It is a curious fact that many conifers that appear in the Jurassic Period seem to be very tall forms in which the vegetation is confined to the very highest branches.

The giant lycopods and horsetails were adapted for life in moist conditions and became extinct in the drier Permian Period. Many of the seed-ferns also became extinct, but a few survived. These were on the whole smaller types with tougher leaves that were better able to cope with the drier conditions. The true ferns, however, which had not been particularly abundant in earlier times, prospered in the new conditions and rose to become the most important ground cover plants of the Mesozoic Era, equivalent to the grasses of today.

The Cordaitales seemed unable to survive the rise of the conifers at the end of the Carboniferous Period and are not found in rocks younger than those of the Permian Period. The conifers (needlepines, firs, spruce, larches, redwoods etc.) spread rapidly once they had appeared in the Late Carboniferous, and became the dominant tree type during much of the Mesozoic Era.

Triassic times and plants

The landscape of the Triassic Period (the first Period of the Mesozoic Era) seems likely to have been arid and perhaps bare of the vegetation in places compared with earlier times. However, there must have been patches of dense vegetation, which showed the beginnings of the vegetational pattern that would become established in the Jurassic Period and which sustained great populations of herbivorous dinosaurs. Two very important newcomers to the plant kingdom appear at this time, the cycads and bennettitaleans (also, confusingly, known as cycadeoids) – both gymnosperms. Bennettitaleans are now completely extinct, but several cycad species have survived in warmer parts of the world.

Above left: *A frond of the cycad* Nilssonia *preserved in Middle Jurassic sandstone from Yorkshire.*

Below left: *A modern cycad with a short trunk and crown of leaves. The dinosaurs that may have fed on such plants in Mesozoic times would have needed tough teeth and a powerful digestive system to cope with the hard, abrasive leaves.*

Above right: *The leaves of the ginkgo are very characteristic, as seen in these fossil examples.*

Below right: *Ginkgos flourished during the Mesozoic Era but there is only one species living today. Ginkgo biloba is a substantial tree that can often be found in the ornamental parks of the world.*

Cycads are squat trees, with stout, often unbranched, trunks that bear a bushy crown of broad leaves, resembling those of palms. Like other gymnosperms, they produce pollen or seed cones from large cones that project from the top of the trunk where all the leaves sprout out. The leaves of these plants are very tough with large amounts of silica in them, which makes them extremely indigestible to most modern animals. This may have been a defence mechanism dating back to the time when dinosaurs were the principal predators of plants.

Bennettitaleans were very like cycads in appearance; they too sprouted a crown of palm frond-like leaves from the top of the trunk, which was often short and squat as in cycads. Some bennettitaleans (for example *Williamsoniella*) had quite tall and branched trunks, however. The main difference between these two groups of plants was in their mode of reproduction. The seeds in bennettitaleans were borne in capsules on the trunk rather than on the crown, which gave the trunks of these plants a distinctively knobbled appearance.

Ginkgos

A type of gymnosperm tree that flourished during the Mesozoic Era, ginkgos are now rare, with only one living representative, *Ginkgo biloba*. These trees had peculiar, particularly distinctive fan-shaped leaves that looked a little like those of flowering trees. Male and female trees were separate, and the pollen was borne on tall cones tucked beneath the leaves. *Ginkgo* itself is a fine example of a living fossil; the same species seems to have been living in the Jurassic Period. Beyond the Jurassic, however, these trees gradually declined, probably reflecting the rise of the flowering plants and trees in the following, Cretaceous, Period.

Ferns, tree ferns and horsetails

Ferns of all types were abundant during the Mesozoic Era, at least in the wetter areas where they thrive today. Delta deposits are often found to contain the rich root and stem beds of horsetails, which tends to suggest that these grew in shallow waters, much as do reeds today. Mesozoic horsetails do not seem to have formed large trees as they did in Carboniferous forests.

While ferns and gymnosperms continued to dominate the world's floras in the Early Cretaceous Period, many varieties of flowering plants were beginning to make their appearance.

FLOWERING PLANTS

Flowering plants – or angiosperms, as they are known, were the last new plants to appear on Earth, and though other types of vegetation continued to exist, were to rise to dominate the floras of the world to later times.

Within 30 million years of the first appearance of flowering plants in the Early Cretaceous Period, land vegetation had been completely transformed. By the end of the Cretaceous, the seed-ferns and bennettitaleans had become extinct, while the cycads and ginkgos had become much less common. The flowering plants or angiosperms (covered seeds) were apparently spreading into the spaces left by the vanishing gymnosperms, and they were also spreading out to colonize new habitats.

Flowering plants as a group are very diverse in habitat and form, ranging from enormous trees, 200ft(60m) or more tall, in tropical rainforests, to scrub acacia in desert conditions, right down to very minute duckweeds that look a little like algae.

The main difference between gymnosperms and angiosperms is in their reproductive structures, that is, the flowers. Flowers can vary enormously: from brightly coloured, intricate shapes (such as those of orchids), designed to be attractive to insects, which inadvertently provide a pollination service; to minute, inconspicuous ones, which are pollinated by wind just as are gymnosperms. However, whether the flowers are highly coloured or not, the seed-producing structure is basically the same. The seeds are totally enclosed and protected in some kind of case, which may be surrounded by a soft fruit.

Angiosperms were able to exploit habitats more efficiently than gymnosperms because of their reproductive advantages. The development of flowers enabled them to use insects as agents to transfer pollen from plant to plant and thereby guarantee fertilization of the seeds; pollination became a much less risky business than when it was solely dependent upon wind. This relationship was made possible by the mutual evolution of insect and plant in such a way that in some cases only one species of insect is involved in the pollination of a single plant species. Apart from being able to produce seeds more reliably and more efficiently, the angiosperms also had a very large competitive advantage when it came to colonizing

new areas of land: in most cases their seeds were able to germinate and grow into new plants in a matter of weeks, rather than months, or even years, as was the case with gymnosperms. The advantage of this system becomes apparent when we consider the pressures under which these plants lived during the Mesozoic Era.

As we have already seen, one of the major factors that affected plants in the Mesozoic Era must have been the large, browsing dinosaurs. Herds of large sauropods, ornithopods or ceratopians would have cut a swathe through the woodlands or forests of their time, leaving devastated areas of land to recover as best they could. Small ferns would have been able to regenerate relatively quickly from the underground root systems, so would not have been so badly affected; the gymnosperm trees, however, would have required a very long time to repopulate an area because of the long time it took for their seeds to germinate and for trees to grow up again from seeds. By contrast, any angiosperms would be able to repopulate the cleared areas fairly rapidly.

It could be, and has been, argued by some palaeontologists that angiosperms were able to evolve because they could exploit the conditions – large areas of open land – created by the activities of herbivorous dinosaurs. The actual cause of the rise of the angiosperms in middle Cretaceous times, and the group of plants from which they have evolved, continue to be mysteries. Nevertheless, by the close of the Cretaceous Period the vegetation was beginning to be dominated by angiosperms of all sorts, ranging from herbs to shrubs and large trees. But one thing that they did not manage to achieve at this time was total domination of the groundcover environment; this was still the preserve of ferns, provided of course that water was nearby.

The Cainozoic plant world

The close of the Cretaceous Period – the last Period of the Mesozoic Era – seemed to show a shift away from the widespread tropical and subtropical climates that had dominated much of the Mesozoic. The climate became progressively more seasonal, favouring hardier varieties of plant and ones that could respond to seasonal conditions, which naturally encouraged the flowering plants. The principal victims of this change were the bennettitaleans and seed-ferns, which did not survive beyond the close of the Cretaceous. Both the ginkgos and horsetails waned, and the conifers, which survived, were a little more restricted in their habitats, continuing mainly as hardy types in colder upland areas.

The decline of all these groups seems to mirror the expansion of the angiosperms. The only really competitive group, as far as this expansion is concerned, was the ferns. About 50 million years ago, however, the grasses evolved. This was the last important group, missing from the Mesozoic Era. Their appearance was probably climatically induced and coincides with a time of cooler, drier conditions and a decline of the forested areas of the world, giving open woodland species the opportunity to establish themselves. Grasses are also closely linked to the evolution of plain-dwelling mammals, especially horses (see pages 18–19).

The Cainozoic addition of the grasses completes the picture of plant evolution during the Phanerozoic Eon. Indeed, most plant species alive today (apart from those that Man had bred artificially) can be traced back to descendants that were living at the very end of the Mesozoic Era, some 64 million years ago.

Far left: *The beautiful magnolia is thought to be one of the most primitive examples of the modern flowering plant group.*

Below: *The expansion of open plains and the spread of the grasses is a dominant theme during the latter part of the Cainozoic Era.*

FORAMINIFERANS AND SPONGES

Among the animals whose fossil remains make up part of the fossil record are a number of rather problematic groups. Some, such as the foraminiferans (see below), straddle the divide between animal and plant kingdoms; others, such as the sponges and now extinct archaeocyathans, are representatives of animal groups that are little like animals at all.

Protistans: foraminiferans
Protistans are microscopically small, single-celled organisms, generally ranging in size from 1 micrometre (one thousandth of a millimetre) to 1 millimetre in diameter (although, as we shall see, there are exceptions.) All protistans are inhabitants of water,

and as a result of their tiny size can exist in small moist places in otherwise very dry areas (on the film of water around sand grains, for example). The group includes many types that are photosynthetic (that is, they possess chemical pigments that allow them to obtain energy from sunlight) and are therefore strictly speaking plants. Here we will look at those that do not photosynthesize and are thus animal-like – protozoans, of which about 20,000 fossil types are known.

The most important group of protozoans are foraminiferans (known as 'forams' for short). These are found in rocks that date from the Cambrian Period (some 570 mya) to recent times, and are found almost exclusively in marine sediments. They range in size from about 0.004–0.02in(0.1–0.5mm) in diameter, but some 'giants' grow up to 6in(15cm) in diameter, which makes them

the largest single-celled organisms known.

The foram's body form is decided by the hard 'test' or chamber in which it lives, and this can be either a single compartment, or may have several chambers. The variation in chemical composition, shape, and ornamentation of the 'test' tend to be very distinctive (useful for identification purposes). The test may be of a wide range of materials, including soft parchmentlike covering (rarely fossilized); foreign material glued on with silica, such as sand grains or tiny shell fragments; or chalky, calcite particles. The latter two types tend to preserve well as fossils. Its shape may be a simple sphere, tubular, flat or cone-shaped spirals, or, sometimes, completely irregular. Whatever its shape, the chamber must have apertures (holes) through which the tissues of the 'foram' can protrude for feeding.

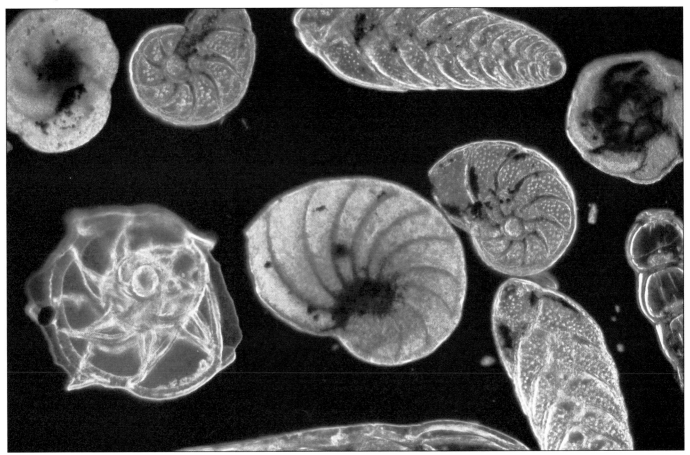

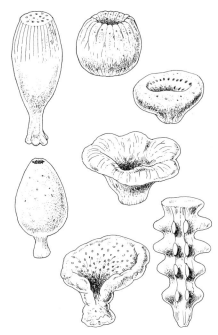

Sponges

Sponges are entirely sessile (unmoving) marine animals. They are more complex than protistans in that they are large-bodied organisms with at least two types of cell, which perform different functions. They have an outer layer of covering cells, which forms a 'skin', and within the thick body wall, special collar cells (choanocytes), which wave a special whiplike thread (flagella) to draw water through the body and filter out microscopic food particles. The skeleton of the body may be of silica (the glass sponges), chalk, or protein threads (the skeleton of a loofah). In the case of the mineralized sponges, the shapes of the individual chalky or silica spicules that make up the skeleton can be very useful for identifying particular species.

The whole body of the sponge is perforated by holes, which tend to be larger near the top of the animal. The bottom of the sponge is cemented to rocks on the sea floor. The exact body shape of a sponge is not constant but tends to adapt to suit the shape of the sea bed and the water currents of the area. The most common shapes are funnels, cups and discs, but spherical, tubular, or irregularly lobed shapes are also known. Some sponges are rock borers, able to split off tiny fragments of rock or shells to create fine branching tunnels.

Left: *A variety of foraminiferans. The chambers of these microscopic organisms are sometimes complex and made of materials such as silica, chalk and sand grains.*

Above: *A section through the centre of a macroforminifer,* Nummulites laevigatus. *This 'giant foram' lived on warm ocean beds, where it formed thick limestone rocks.*

Above: *Sponges vary enormously in shape: this selection, ranges in age from the Devonian to the Cretaceous Period.*

Below: *A fossilized example of an early sponge,* Raphidoneura. *Its shape adapted to suit the contours of the sea bed.*

The overwhelming majority of foraminiferans inhabit the sea. Most are mobile bottom-dwellers though some, especially the irregularly shaped ones, are fixed. A few live at the ocean surface. The distribution of the bottom-living forms is strongly affected by water temperature, and they are therefore very useful indicators of ancient oceanic temperatures.

Several different types of foraminiferan are known: macroforaminifers include (as the name suggests) giant forms and were particularly common in the Late Carboniferous and Permian Periods, as well as in the Late Cretaceous and Early Tertiary. Macroforaminifers appear to have been bottom-dwelling forms, which lived in warm ocean waters and formed many of the thick limestone rocks of these periods. Some living relatives are known today in coral reefs of the tropical oceans. Many of the disc, lens or spindle-shaped 'macroforams' are excellent marker fossils for dating rocks. Among the more common species are *Fusilina, Schwagerina, Alveolina, Nummulites, Orbitoides, Discocyclina* and *Lepidocyclina*).

ARCHAEOCYATHANS

Archaeocyathans are a peculiar group of fossils that look like sponges. They also bear some similarity to corals (see page 36), but at present palaentologists do not entirely agree about the origins of this group. Archaeocyathans first appeared in Early Cambrian times (about 600mya) but were entirely extinct by the late Cambrian (about 500mya). Because of this relatively narrow time range and their apparent rapid evolution, the archaeocyathans are particularly useful for ageing rocks from different parts of the world.

Their chalky skeleton is shaped like that of a cup-sponge and riddled with holes, like a sieve. They tend to be sharply conical and no more than about 0.8in(20mm) in diameter and 4.7in(120mm) long and the body seems to consist of a two-layer wall enclosing a central space. The inner and outer walls are connected by regularly spaced radiating walls, each of which, again, is highly perforated.

Archaeocyathans were fixed forms, living on the sea floor, to which they attached themselves with a rootlike disc, in shallow tropical seas. Judging from the rocks in which they are found, they appear to have preferred depths of 65–130ft(20–40m), only smaller forms living above or below this range of depths. In the Early Cambrian Period, archaeocyathans formed dense reefs in association with algae; these fossil assemblages (or groupings) are found particularly in Eastern USSR, Africa, Australia and North America.

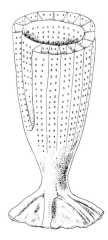

Left: *The cylindrical upper body of this archaeocyathan was attached to the ocean floor by a rootlike holdfast. Despite the striking resemblance, it is not related to the sponges.*

Below: *Protopharetra, an example of a fossil archaeocyathan from Georgia, USSR. Fossil groupings of algae and archaeocyathans have also been found in Africa, Australia and North America.*

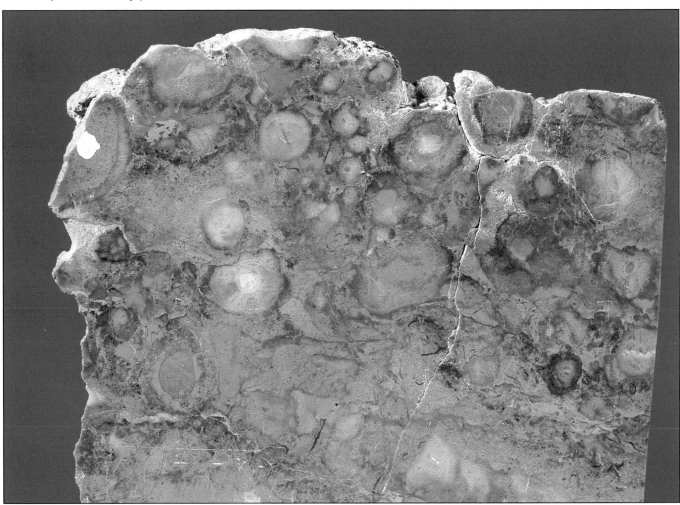

MYSTERY ANIMALS

The earliest animals that did more than simply sit on the sea floor sieving sea water as both the sponges and archaeocyathans seem to have done, were first found in Late Proterozoic rocks (approximately 630 million years old) in the Ediacara Hills of South Australia in 1947. Since that time similar faunas have been found elsewhere in the world and are known as 'ediacaran' faunas. Many resemble living animals; for example, *Glaesnerina* (sea pens) – tall, slender, coral-like forms and *Mawsonites* (probable jelly fish). Other forms are more puzzling and have no obvious present-day equivalents; for example, *Dickinsonia* and *Spriggina*, both of which were curious wormlike types.

Somewhat younger deposits from mid-Cambrian rocks of British Columbia, Canada, have also revealed some very interesting active animals. This Burgess Shale fauna was apparently preserved in mud-slides from, as it is now known, underwater cliffs and includes a remarkable variety of forms. Again, some are clearly comparable to species living today or to others that appear later in the fossil record. They include trilobites (*Olenoides*), the shrimp like *Waptia*, and various types of worm, such as representatives of bristle worms (*Canadia*).

In addition, the Burgess Shale fauna includes a variety of extremely strange creatures that seem to represent evolutionary experiments in animal design. *Opabinia*, for example, was a strange, wormlike form that evidently walked or swam on fleshy lobes projecting from the sides of the body, and had a long protrusible trunk used for catching its prey. But perhaps the most peculiar of all was the aptly named *Hallucigenia*, the like of which has never been seen before nor since. This strange beast had seven pairs of spinelike legs, seven soft tentacles waving from its back, a slender tail, and a bulbous head with no mouth! Clusters of these creatures have been found on rocky layers around what may be carcasses of dead animals, which suggests that they may have been scavengers.

One other interesting animal of the Burgess Shale, *Pikaia* is possibly an early chordate (see pages 48–9), and may have been a very early ancestor of all the later vertebrates. Unfortunately, deposits showing soft-bodied animals such as the Ediacaran and the Burgess Shale fauna are few;

palaeontologists receive only a rare glimpse of the early evolution of most active animal groups. During the Cambrian Period, however, an increasing number of animal groups began to develop hard, shelly skeletons, which naturally preserve better.

Above: *This shrimplike organism,* Waptia fieldensis, *has been preserved in fine-grained muds some 530 million years old.*

Below: Hallucigenia, *an aptly named and extraordinary creature from the Burgess Shale deposits, has no living counterpart.*

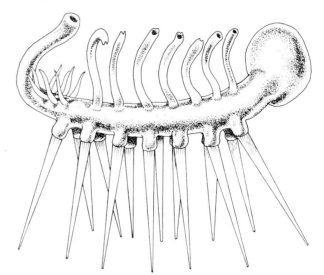

COELENTERATES

The group known as coelenterates includes the corals, anenomes and jellyfish, most of which are marine. All these animals have a soft elastic body, with a single opening for food to pass in, and for waste to pass out. Coelenterates are surprisingly accomplished predators. Their 'mouth' is surrounded by a ring of tentacles, which are covered by tiny knobbly bumps (visible under a microscope). These bumps mark the position of explosive capsules, which burst open when they sense prey nearby, firing a long, sharp thread, to pierce the body of the prey and inject a paralyzing poison. Once the prey is paralyzed, the flexible body of the coelenterate stretches and the mouth expands enormously to engulf the prey, which is held in the stomach while it is slowly digested.

Coelenterates can be divided into a number of different types, depending on their way of life and body form:

Hydrozoans live in colonies surrounded by a horny protein coat. While abundant in recent communities, they are relatively rare in the fossil record.

Scyphozoans include free-floating jellyfish. It is suspected that jellyfish remains are preserved in the Ediacara fauna, which would make them a very ancient group, but their remains are otherwise extremely rare. Another group of scyphozoans are the conulates, which are wholly extinct. They are found in rocks dating from between the middle of the Cambrian and the Triassic. Conulates are preserved as fossils in the form of square-based pyramids with finely ridged sides. Flap-shaped extensions of the base of these containers may have served as a lid for the animal. Most conulates seem to have lived on the sea floor and were attached by the pointed end. Their tentacles probably spread upward and outward. Some conulates seem to have drifted pointed end upward, trailing their tentacles through the plankton to catch small creatures.

Anthozoans – a group that includes corals and sea anemones – are rather like hydrozoans in that they are bottom dwellers, living mostly in huge sprawling colonies. They, too, develop skeletons of tough protein or of chalk and lime, but they have far more complicated stomachs, which are divided into many chambers.

The anthozoans play the most important part in the fossil record of these coelenterate groups because they are reef builders of the warm oceans. The limey cups, or skeletons, of the dead members ('polyps') of the colony form huge masses of limestone, while the living polyps form a thin skin on the surface of the reef. When threatened, disturbed, or exposed to too much sunlight, these living polyps can retract into the limestone cup for protection. The limestone cups preserve very well as fossils and can be traced back to the Ordovician Period (440–500 mya). Anthozoans existed before this time, but seem not to have mastered the technique of glueing themelves to the sea bed and so could not form huge, reeflike masses. Many had pointed bases and must have drifted about on the sea floor.

In addition to the colonial types, there were (and still are) solitary forms of anthozoan; these build up a conical stack of limestone as they become larger, and form distinctive irregular, conical shapes.

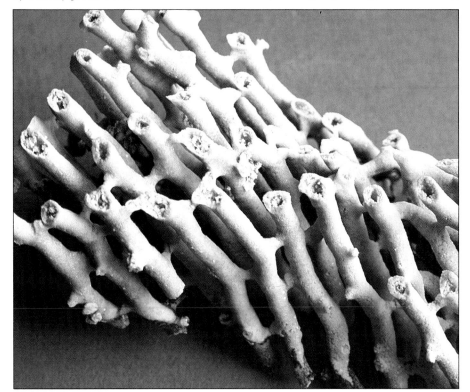

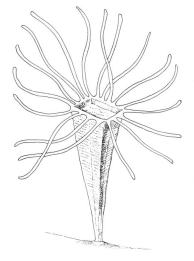

Left: Syringopora, *a fossil hydrozoan, shows the tubular skeleton in which colonies of these small creatures lived. The tubes interconnect, so that all members are in communication.*

Above: *A conulate. These small (two-to-five-centimetre-long) fossils had grooved angular sides and a chevron-shaped external surface. This one shows a tentacled rim and holdfast.*

BRACHIOPODS

Brachiopods, or lamp shells, are among the most common of all fossils and can be found in rocks ranging in age from 600 million years to present day. Several hundred species live in the ocean today, but these are only a tiny remnant of the 30,000 species known to have lived in the past. The greatest proportion of fossil brachiopods lived in the Palaeozoic Era, but they underwent a huge decline at the end of the Permian Period, from which they never fully recovered.

Brachiopods are marine animals, living on the sea bed, to which they are normally attached by a short tail (or pedicle). Most live on hard surfaces, but some have the ability to anchor themselves, or live in burrows in mud. The soft parts of the body are protected and supported by a shell with two valves. The valves are either jointed very poorly (in the case of *inarticulate* brachiopods) or have a well developed hinge (*articulate* brachiopods). The body is quite small and sits at the back of the shell cavity (near the hinge), the remainder of the space being taken up by an enormously complex tentacled sieving mechanism, which is known as *lophophore*.

When the valves of the shell are opened, tiny brushlike hairs beat and draw water through the shell cavity from the sides, passing it out at the front. As the water passes through the cavity, microscopic food particles are strained out on the lophophore, and are passed back to the mouth along special grooves. Special muscles open and close the valves of the shell, and muscles in the pedicle allow the shell to reposition itself from time to time.

Shells of most brachiopods are between one and five centimetres long or wide and are composed of tough protein (chitin), which may be mixed with calcium phosphate (in the case of inarticulate brachiopods) or calcite (in the case of articulate ones). Both valves are usually domed, but some have flat or concave upper valves or, more rarely, similarly shaped lower valves.

The details of the shape of the valves, of the hinge line, and the structure of the hinge itself, as well as the area for the valve-closing muscles, are very important characteristics for distinguishing brachiopod species. (The internal structure of the hinge and the supporting skeleton for the lophophore are also important, but can often only be studied by making cut sections of the fossils.)

Right: *One of a wide variety of brachiopods, this type,* spirifer, *is characterized by a rathe short shell (top to bottom) and a nearly flat hinge area. The feeding arms of this species are coiled into spirals, which extend out into the pointed (upper) corners of the shell.*

Above: Lingula. *One of the most long-lived of all animal groups, these brachiopods show little change in outward appearance from the Cambrian Period through to the present day. The thin shell is strengthened by thin layers of calcium phosphate and collagen.*

Many brachiopods seem to have become adapted to particular types of environment, and quite often their form is a reflection of the environmental conditions. For example, some brachiopod communities of the Silurian Period seem to be fossilized in bands running more or less parallel with the ancient shoreline. Each band of brachiopods would seem to be adapted to a particular depth of water, or type of feeding area. Living brachiopods inhabit cool waters, but in the Palaeozoic Era they lived in various conditions on the sea bed. One of the largest brachiopods is found in the Carboniferous Period: *Gigantoproductus*, which reached a diameter of 20in(50cm).

Towards the end of the Permian Period the brachiopods suffered an almost catastrophic decline in abundance (along with many other groups of marine organisms). The few groups that survived include the rhynchonellids and terebratulids, which became very abundant during the Jurassic Period. It would appear that the colonization of the muddy sea floor after the Permian was largely taken over by the similar, but more versatile bivalve molluscs. Living brachiopods are still quite abundant in the shallow waters of the Pacific and Indian Ocean (some are even to be found around the coast of Britain), but they are vastly outnumbered by the variety of bivalve molluscs.

MOLLUSCS

Some molluscs (the bivalves) look a little like brachiopods, but the likeness is due to a similarity of lifestyle, rather than because the groups are actually related. The structure of the body and organs and the composition of the shell of bivalve molluscs are, in fact, very different from those of brachiopods.

In simple terms, molluscs consist of a head with a mouth, which may have jaws or a strip of horny teeth on a short tongue, and a bulbous body, beneath which there is a large muscular foot. A thin fleshy mantle forms an umbrellalike covering to much of the body and a shell protects this mantle. The earliest mollusc fossils are very small hat-shaped shells, which come from the early Cambrian of Russia. They are some of the simplest of all molluscs and belong to a group known as monoplacophorans. The only living representative of this group – *Neopilina* – was dredged up from the ocean depths for the first time in 1957.

After the appearance of these first hat-shaped molluscs there seems to have been a trend towards a change in shape of the shell (and of course the underlying body organs) in two principal directions. One group is characterized by the formation of taller, more pointed shells so that the body became 'hunched' into the pointed end. This type eventually gave rise to such familiar forms as gastropod snails, ammonites and squids (see pages 40–1). The other types tended to develop narrower hat-shaped shells, as though the rim of the 'hat' had been folded down at the sides. This group, which we will look at first, gave rise to the bivalve molluscs.

Bivalve molluscs

Bivalves are almost always equally divided into two along the line of the valves. The body is located alongside the hinge area with the head at one end and the tail at the other. A slim muscular foot, which can be used for movement along the sea bed when pushed out between the valves into the sediment, is tucked up beneath the body behind the head. The valves are held together by muscles located at either end of the shell, and these work against a ligament inside the hinge, which tends to pull the valves apart. As the muscles relax, the valves gape and feeding can start.

As in the brachiopods, much of the chamber inside the shell is occupied by folded sieving membranes covered with tiny tufts of hair, which beat and draw water and particles of food into the shell. The food particles are trapped on the surface of the sieving

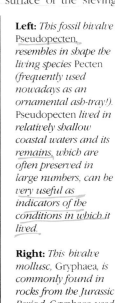

Left: *This fossil bivalve* Pseudopecten, *resembles in shape the living species* Pecten *(frequently used nowadays as an ornamental ash-tray!).* Pseudopecten *lived in relatively shallow coastal waters and its remains, which are often preserved in large numbers, can be very useful as indicators of the conditions in which it lived.*

Right: *This bivalve mollusc,* Gryphaea, *is commonly found in rocks from the Jurassic Period.* Gryphaea *used to be called 'devil's toe nails' by quarrymen and rural village people earlier this century. The derivation of the name is obvious, reflecting the curiously assymetrical way in which the two valves have grown. The upper valve forms a flat 'door', the lower the main body chamber.*

membrane – the 'gill' – and guided by tiny channels to the mouth. Larger sand grains are rejected and either carried out on the flow of water, or occasionally 'coughed' out from between the valves if there is a danger of the chamber becoming clogged.

All bivalve molluscs live in water, mostly in the sea, living on the sea floor, either attached by threads produced by the foot (mussels, for example), or lying loosely on the surface. Some, such as cockles and clams, live within the sea bed itself, using the foot like a piston to burrow through the mud, dragging the shell after it. Other molluscs are able to use the edges of the valves as 'teeth' in order to burrow into soft rocks on the sea shore, while yet others burrow into timber – a great menace to timber boats.

The hinge is quite complicated, with pegs and sockets to make the joint strong and prevent it becoming dislocated in life. Dif-ferences in the arrangement of these pegs and sockets in the hinge are used to disting-uish different species.

The oldest known bivalves, from the early Cambrian age, are tiny – only just over 1mm long. Even at this early stage (not long after the appearance of the very first molluscs), they have valves and hinges, but they are not very well developed and it is suspected that these tiny bivalves simply sat on the sea bed and filtered food in suspension from the water. By the Ordovician Period, the hinge structure was much more sophisticated and suggests that by this time bivalves had be-come adept burrowers.

From the Palaeozoic Era onwards, bivalves are found abundantly in marine rocks. The shells are made of layers of protein interspersed with mineral layers of calcite or aragonite, which makes them both hard and tough, and therefore excellent items for fossilization. This, combined with the fact that most bivalves live in the shallow seas surrounding continents makes them of immense value to palaeontologists; by chart-ing their occurrence at different periods of time it is possible to map out the margins of ancient continents. Bivalves tend to be rather choosy about the substrates they live upon, and so they also enable palaeontolo-gists to build up a detailed view of the marine environments in ancient seas.

Unlike the bivalves, other mollusc types took to a creeping way of life, using the foot literally to walk with. The shape of the shell changed from a simple conical chinaman's hat shape to one that was more pointed. In some cases, the pointed end of the shell became coiled so that the shell became more compact. Various types of mollusc evolved from this type, the most important of which are gastropods and cephalopods.

Gastropods

Gastropods are perhaps one of the most successful of mollusc groups since they have managed to colonize sea water, fresh water and land habitats. The great majority have a very distinctively coiled chalky shell. The head carries two pairs of flexible sensory tentacles, on the ends of which are mounted inkspot-like eyes, while in the mouth are horny jaws and an abrasive tongue, or, 'radula'. The foot forms a wide, flat, creeping sole, which is lubricated by sticky mucus.

The form of the shell in gastropods varies enormously, but is usually a tapering spiral with varying degrees of overlap between each spiral turn; thus some are low and conical, such as those of top-shells from the sea shore, while others are long, ornate spires, such as those of the many types of whelk. Some have flat coiled shells and look very much like ammonites, others have no spirals at all; the limpet with its simple conical shell, for example.

Classification of fossil gastropods can be problematical for the palaeontologist. Modern zoologists, who have living gastropods to work with, use the soft parts of the animals for classification: the structure of the gills, the nervous system and the patterns of horny teeth on the tongue. Obviously this sort of system will not work for fossil material, so palaeontologists have to be guided by the shape of the shell and its chemical composition. Fortunately, many living species have fossil relatives.

Gastropods are divided into three major groups: prosobranchs, opisthobranchs and pulmonates. Prosobranchs include the most ancient gastropods and date back to the late Cambrian. Nearly all are marine, reflecting the primitive habitat of gastropods. Opisthobranchs include a variety of forms that live in the sea, and have tended to reduce or lose the shell. Some are even capable of underwater flight! Pulmonates are the gastropods that have been able to invade the land. Instead of gills they have lungs, or an air sac, for breathing air. Most inhabit dry land, though some, such as pond snails, have returned to fresh or brackish water.

Below: *The tapering, flat spiral shape of this shell indicate that it belongs to the group of gastropod molluscs.*

The species is Euomphalus pentagulus, *which lived from the Silurian to the Permian Periods.*

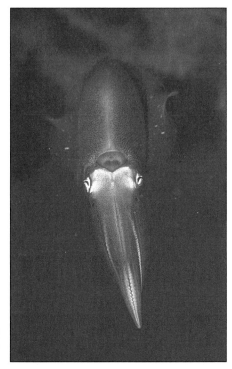

Cephalopods

These are the most mobile of all molluscs and include such extremely fast and highly intelligent swimmers as modern squids, cuttlefish and octopuses. All these forms have long tentacles, which are derived from the molluscan foot, and soft flexible bodies with little external sign of the typical hard mollusc shell. A special muscular funnel is used to create a directional form of jet propulsion in these animals. Most are active hunters of other sea creatures; only a few, such as the pearly nautilus, are known to scavenge dead animals occasionally.

Fossil cephalopods are very diverse and have a strong external shell, especially the ammonoids (ammonites), and these, because of their fine preservation, are excellent for use in aging rocks. Ammonites are found in rocks that date from Devonian times through to the very end of the Creta-ceous Period (about 65mya), when they suddenly and mysteriously became extinct.

Ammonite shells are tubular and arranged in a tight, flat spiral, though a few are nearly straight, or irregularly coiled (particularly those of the late Cretaceous Period). The shell is often very distinctively marked with ridges, furrows or knobs and these aid in classification. As ammonites grew, they gradually moved into larger chambers, which were added to the end of the spiral. The smaller chambers that they left as they grew were filled with gas produced by the ammonite, which aided buoyancy. Each chamber is marked off from its neighbour by a partition or 'septum'. While some ammonites may have a simple flat septum, the majority have extremely complex, folded septa and detailed study of these has proved valuable for sorting out the evolution of the group.

Ammonites seem to have been slow-moving forms, probably living close to the sea floor, or migrating within the water column as do living nautilus. They fed on small organisms (foraminiferans, crinoids and smaller ammonites).

Belemnites

These bullet-shaped fossils ('thunder bolts') are all that remains of the body of squidlike creatures that flourished in the seas from Devonian to recent times. The fossil formed the axis of the body of the animal and is composed of radially arranged prisms of calcite around a fine central core and built up in a series of concentric layers.

Belemnites were very probably fast, cruising swimmers, comparable to modern squids in life style. Their abundant remains in Jurassic and Cretaceous rocks makes them useful for ageing other fossils, as are their cousins, the ammonites.

Above left: *Squids have a fairly poor fossil record because their skeleton consists of a thin ribbon of collagen that runs the length of the body, and this tends to rot with the rest of the body when the animal dies.*

Below left:
Belemnites are close relatives of the living squids but had a strong, bullet-shaped internal skeleton. These fossils (which are also known as 'thunder bolts') can be extremely abundant.

Right: *The cut section through the body of this ammonite shows the way in which these creatures grew. Starting in the middle, the animal grew until it was too large for its chamber, it then grew a larger one, closing of the old one with a partition wall. The empty chambers filled with gas and aided buoyancy.*

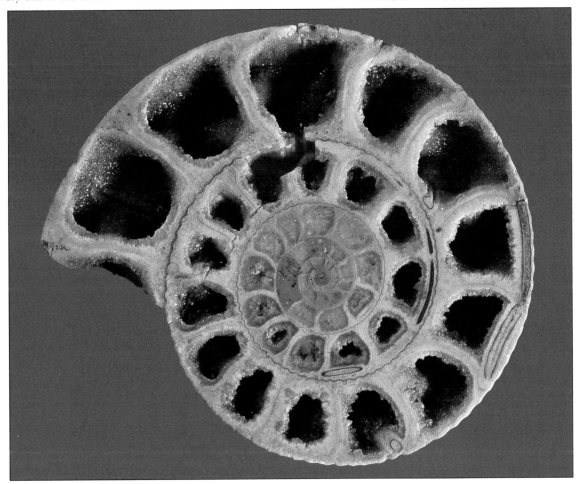

ARTHROPODS

Arthropods are characterized by their segmented body, which tends to have a chitinous covering, or remnants of this, attached by muscles on the inner surface. Originally inhabitants of the sea, some members have very successfully adapted to life on dry land, and in the air.

Annelids are another group worth mentioning here. Despite their outward differences in appearance from arthropods, they are related, albeit distantly. These creatures with soft, segmented bodies are the true worms and include the varieties that are found in garden soil, among other places. The few that are found as fossils are the serpulids, or 'featherduster' worms. They live in tubular burrows made underwater of lime and have a fan of tentacles, which they use to sieve the water for microscopic food.

Arthropod means literally 'jointed leg' and today, this group includes such familiar animals as insects, spiders, crabs and shrimps. The bodies of these creatures are encased in an armour, which may be made of tough fibrous material, such as chitin, or reinforced with chalk or bone, which means that they are frequently fossilized.

Instead of being regularly segmented like a worm, the body of an arthropod is usually divided into a head, body and abdomen, each of which consists of several fused segments. Complex joints between these different sections allow movement. The hard body wall cannot grow along its edges, so these animals periodically shed their skin and grow a new and larger one. Arthropods are divided into the following very distinctive groups.

Trilobites

The trilobites are commonly found as fossils in rocks that range in age from the middle of the Cambrian Period through to the late Permian Period. Trilobites are characterized by a long flattened body, rather like that of a woodlouse, except that it is divided into three lengthwise rows of segments by a pair of grooves that run down the back. The head tends to be a broad shieldlike structure, upon which are perched two multi-lensed eyes. The legs are paired and jointed and are attached to each of the body segments and the tail is usually a flattened plate. The body shell of these animals was made of calcite. Very often the preserved remains of trilobites prove to be the shed skins.

These animals were clearly complex creatures, rather than primitive forms of life. Their many legs would have been moved in rhythm as they scuttled across the sea floor and they probably fed upon tiny organisms living in the mud, or by scavenging. Like the pill ball woodlouse, some trilobites possessed the ability to roll into a ball when danger threatened. Some smaller species seem to have been adept swimmers, with quite streamlined bodies, and broader, paddlelike legs. Trackways of trilobites are occasionally preserved and these give a clear indication of how they moved. Some seem to have walked upon the tips of their limbs, others ploughed through the mud, and yet others show the ability to move sideways, crablike, across the sea floor.

The range and variety of trilobites found in rocks from the Cambrian through to the Permian is great. Some of the earliest trilobites have been found in the Burgess Shales, which reveal a surprisingly diverse range of early trilobite-like creatures.

One of the largest trilobites is *Paradoxides* from the middle Cambrian of Newfoundland, which grew to 12in(30cm) or more in length (most trilobites range in size from 0.8–4in/2–10cm). One rather unusual group of trilobites are the agnostids, many of which come from the late Cambrian. Agnostids are small forms, with only a few segments to the body, and head and tail shields of approximately the same size. This, combined with the fact that many species lack eyes, makes it very difficult to tell one end from the other! Small blind trilobites such as these must have ploughed through the mud of the sea floor, where a sense of touch and taste would have been much more important than vision. Another wellknown trilobite is *Phacops* from the middle Devonian Period, examples of which are often preserved curled up in a ball.

The decline and disappearance of trilobites is a mystery, but they seem to have suffered the fate of many marine animals that also became extinct at the end of the Permian Period.

Below: *This trilobite,* Trinucleus fimbriatus, *is from the Ordovician Period of Wales. These creatures spent their lives scuttling over the sea floor scooping up detritus (rotting animal and vegetable remains). They form exceptionally good fossils due to their hard external skeleton, but many fossils are in fact shed skins rather than the whole animal.*

Chelicerates

The next major group of arthropod fossils are known scientifically as the chelicerates and includes the 'antique' horseshoe crabs, giant 'sea scorpions', spiders, mites and true scorpions. Compared to the trilobites, which tended to be passive, bottom-dwelling mud-grubbers, the chelicerates are much more varied, both in body shape and lifestyle, and include some devastating predatory types.

Horseshoe crabs are extremely ancient members of this group, whose ancestry can be traced back to the early Cambrian Period. They are characterized by a very large, domed shield at the front, which forms a prominent 'head' to the animal, and in which are embedded two multi-lensed eyes. Immediately behind the shield is a short, jointed body, followed by a long, spinelike tail. The first legs are clawed and used for manipulating food, the following four also clawed, are used for walking along the sea floor. The sixth pair are tucked back and used for cleaning the gills. In some species this pair of legs are paddlelike and are used for swimming.

The living horseshoe crab, *Limulus*, of the Pacific Ocean is little different from the earliest of these creatures and is one of a number of puzzling species, such as *Lingula* (the brachiopod) that have hardly changed over hundreds of millions of years.

Eurypterids, or giant 'sea scorpions', are relatives of the horseshoe crabs that ranged in time from the Ordovician until the Permian Period, and in size, from a few inches to six and a half feet (two metres) long. By comparison with horseshoe crabs they had long, stretched bodies and seem to have been adapted to swimming above the sea floor. A few actively hunted for prey.

Eurypterus, from the Silurian Period, had small claws, and four pairs of tufted legs, which do not seem particularly well adapted for walking; the sixth legs were modified into large paddles. This species was very probably a free-swimming scavenger. *Pterygotus*, of the early Devonian Period, was a very large form, sometimes reaching lengths of nearly seven feet. This was one of the most accomplished of early sea predators; its first claws were very long and ended in large pincers, with sawlike teeth, which it used for capturing and tearing apart its prey. Like *Eurypterus*, *Pterygotus* had large sixth swimming paddles and a long tail, but in the latter species, this tail ended in a flattened paddle.

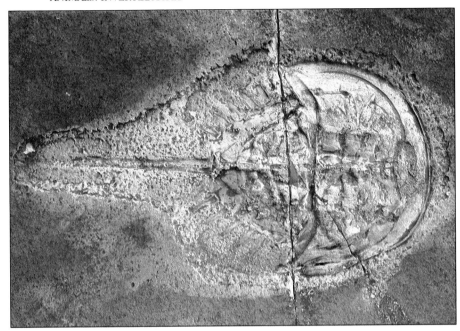

A flick of this tail would have generated a sharp burst of speed, which would have enabled it to attack prey. *Pterygotus* was one of the largest invertebrates that has ever lived, and could have eaten any other creature alive in its time. (It's modern equivalent would be something like a killer whale!)

Other eurypterids included *Carcinosoma*, a fat-bodied form with a venom-carrying tail spine, and *Stylonura*, which crept along the sea floor on long spindly legs.

By the end of the Carboniferous Period, all the large eurypterids had disappeared from the seas, their place being taken by large predatory fish. The remaining forms were smaller and began to inhabit brackish water and streams, but despite this move to new and different habitats, they, too, became extinct at the end of the Permian Period.

Arachnids (the group that includes spiders and scorpions) is an interesting group, whose ancestry goes back to the Silurian Period, but unfortunately is rarely represented in the fossil record. Arachnids are mainly land-living forms, whose bodily remains would normally have been destroyed by the processes of decay long before they had the chance to enter the erosional cycle that produces fossils (see pages 10–11). Some spiders and scorpions have been beautifully preserved in the Tertiary amber from the Baltic.

Above: *Horseshoe crabs have an extensive fossil record. This example, Mesolimulus, is from the Jurassic Period.*

Below: *This is a finely preserved example of a water scorpion from the Silurian Period, Eurypterus. Note the large paddles.*

Mandibulates

Mandibulates are another important group of arthropods which have dominated waters, land and air from the Cambrian Period to recent times. The group is comprised mainly of crustaceans and insects.

Crustaceans

These mandibulates are predominantly water dwellers, only some of which are important as fossils. We will look at the most significant fossil crustaceans here.

Conchostracans are small, bivalved creatures that live in freshwater. When found in reasonable numbers they can help to date rocks of otherwise unknown age.

Ostracods are also small bivalved creatures, which resemble water fleas (*Daphnia*). They show many parallel developments in the structure of the complex hinge and ligaments to those of some bivalve molluscs, but the animal that inhabits this shell is completely different. Like conchostracans, ostracods have been used extensively, for comparatively dating rocks, and, since most of these marine creatures prefer to live on the deep sea floor, they are also useful as indicators of the environmental conditions that existed when the rocks were formed.

Barnacles (*Cirripedia*) are generally small and either live attached to rocks (or, more rarely, to algae) or may be highly specialized parasites even attaching themselves to large

Above: *This is a good example of a typical decapod crustacean – a shrimp. The long tail ends in a flat fan, which can be flexed to produce a rapid backward motion.*

Below: *Ostracods, such as* Euphorberia, *shown here, are small bivalved creatures that generally live in plankton and can be used as index markers of particular strata.*

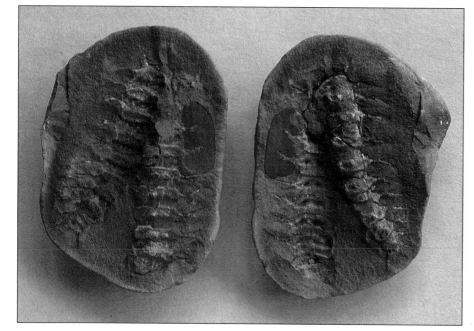

swimming vertebrates. Goose barnacles (stalked barnacles) and acorn barnacles (the more familiar ones seen encrusting rocks on the sea shore) are important invertebrates that have existed since Cambrian times. The arrangement of the chalky plates that form the homes for these creatures are useful in their identification.

The other major group of crustaceans are the malacostracans, characterized by the way their bodies are divided up into regions. The head region and thorax are usually covered by an armoured casing (known as the cephalothorax), from which legs and claws project. Behind this is the abdomen, whose smaller legs are sometimes modified to form gills, or, in the smaller aquatic swimmers, may be used as paddles. Most malacostracans live in the sea, but some inhabit fresh water and a few have become terrestrial. Crabs, lobsters, shrimps and woodlice all belong to this group.

The most abundant fossil remains of malacostracans are those of the decapods, found in rocks that range in age from the late Permian Period through to recent times. Instead of having eight pairs of walking or swimming legs on the cephalothorax, decapods have only five, the first three pairs having become modified into accessory feeding legs that surround the mouth and manipulate food for the jaws. The first pair of the main walking legs frequently carry very large claws. The majority of decapods have a long tail, the end of which is often developed into a broad fan that can be flexed downward and forward to produce a rapid backward swimming movement, but there are also forms known in which the abdomen is reduced and which lack a distinct tail. The decapods abdomen is either soft and curved, to fit into a mollusc shell (as in hermit crabs), or is flattened and tucked up against the cephalothorax (as in crabs). It seems that during the evolution of the decapods, short-tailed forms have evolved from long-tailed varieties on a number of occasions, so that short-tailed decapods may not be as closely related to one another as they appear.

Woodlice incubate their young in chambers between their legs and this has enabled them to colonize land. They are the only really successful land-dwelling crustaceans; land crabs are successful in some places, particularly oceanic islands where competition with larger (potentially predatory) animals is restricted, but land crabs still have to return to the sea to mate.

Centipedes and millipedes (grouped scientifically as 'myriapods') are unfortunately rather rare as fossils. The best remains have been found in Baltic and South American amber. Numerous tracks have also been found in rocks ranging from the Devonian Period through to recent times, which resemble those left by modern forms.

Problematic arthropods

There are numerous arthropods known in the fossil record, particularly those from the Palaeozoic Era, that do not fit readily into the known living groups of arthropods. One notable species is *Arthropleura* a gigantic – up to six and a half foot – arthropod from the Late Carboniferous Period. *Arthropleura* had a rather flattened body and looked like a millipede, but its many legs more closely resembled those of a trilobite. These gigantic animals seem to have lived in the leaf-litter on the floor of Carboniferous forests. The stomach contents of one such animal indicate that clubmosses were an important part of the diet of this species.

Mimetaster from the Early Devonian Period is another problem species. It has an extraordinary starlike upper shell (or 'carapace') and an array of long front legs and short rear ones. The way of life of this marine animal is a mystery, but it may have been a scavenger of dead creatures, using its spikey armour as protection against predators while feeding.

Insects

The first true insects make their appearance in the Devonian Period. They are characterized by the body, which is divided into three segments – a head, thorax and abdomen – and by their six legs – one pair on each of the three segments of the thorax. Winged insects develop two pairs of wings, on the second and third segments of the thorax, though many insects only use one pair. Beetles, for example, use the first wings as wingcases to protect the delicate second wings while they move about on land, whereas many flies use the first pair only, the second being reduced to small drumsticklike structures called 'halteres', which they appear to use as stabilizers and wing-beat controllers in flight.

Being mostly landliving, insects have developed their own curious breathing system, called a tracheal system. A row of holes along the sides of the body (a pair in each segment) can be covered by valves and lead into a network of fine tubes. Body movements pump air in and out of the body through these tubes.

The mouthparts of insects vary enormously, and, depending on their feeding habits, are adapted for biting, piercing or sucking.

Although insects account for about three-quarters of all living species, they have a relatively poor fossil record. Most are small, rendering the chance of their being found slight; they live on land or in the air, neither of which is conducive to the process of fossilization, and their bodies are made of tough protein (chitin), which, though hard, tends to rot and therefore preserves poorly. Nevertheless, insects are known to date back to at least the Late Silurian Period, when evidence is found of damage to early plants that was probably caused by sap-sucking insects. Carboniferous insects include a host of cockroach types and dragonflies, some of which, such as *Meganeura*, grew to enormous size (30in/76cm wingspan).

In recent years more interest has been taken in the part insects play in the fossil record as detailed work on fine rocks has begun to reveal large numbers, especially in the Cretaceous Period, the time when flowering plants evolved, many of which rely upon insects for pollination.

Below: *Insects are rarely found as fossils because of their fragile bodies. This dragonfly,* *trapped in fine lake sediments, has been exceptionally well preserved.*

ECHINODERMS & GRAPTOLITES

Echinoderms, distinctive because of their five-fold symmetry, are represented today by creatures such as starfish and sea urchins and are common as fossils. Graptolites become extinct at the end of the Carboniferous Period.

Echinoderms

Starfish, urchins and sand dollars, sea lilies and sea cucumbers are all included in this very distinctive group of creatures. Modern ones all possess five-fold symmetry of the body, which is a most unusual feature in the animal kingdom, and lack a distinctive front end. They are either slow-moving, or stationary animals, entirely confined to sea water, and have a chalky type of body skeleton, which can be rigid, or quite flexible. These creatures move largely by means of a unique water-vascular system – a system of water-filled tubes forming a network through the body, which operates hundreds of small tube-feet. The tube-feet are highly mobile and end in small suckers or are shaped like tentacles. Because of their chalky skeleton, echinoderms are frequently found as fossils; their fossil record extends back to the Early Cambrian Period, and they seem to have been most abundant and varied in the Palaeozoic Era.

There are four modern types of echinoderm: crinoids (sea lilies), asteroids (starfish), echinoids (sea urchins) and holothuroids (sea cucumbers), but 17 other, now extinct classes of echinoderm once existed, showing a bewildering variety of forms. Here we will look at a sample of the most important fossil echinoderms.

Homalozoans are small, extinct Palaeozoic forms (Cambrian to Devonian). They are notable for their asymmetric shape; the body is usually flattened and consists of a roughly rounded broad end (the 'theca') and a stalk (the 'stele' or tail). The theca is made up of plates of calcite; the peripheral ones seem to have been rigid, whereas those in the centre were flexible. Homalozoans seem to have lived on the sea floor, dragging themselves around on the sand or mud using the flexible tail or stalk. Some homalozoans are thought to have been the ancestors of chordates (see pages 48–9) because of the similarities in the form of the globular body (with gills) and the long tail, which is also seen in living chordates.

Blastozoans, which first made their appearance in the Middle Cambrian and became extinct during the Permian Period, tend to be either spherical or bagshaped with short armlike brachioles. Quite often these forms were attached to the sea floor by a stalk and many had five-fold symmetry. Blastozoans vary a great deal; some are a little like crinoids, others are globular or spherical with short or absent stalks, while others tend to have longer stalks, short bodies and fine clusters of brachioles, and are more symmetrical in shape.

Crinozoans range from small to 20 metres long and have existed from Ordovician times through to the present. Again, the body is usually five-fold symmetrical. Most are attached by a long stem to the substrate or, more rarely, cemented to the surface, but in the Mesozoic Era a few mobile ones appeared and these types are still found today in shallow seas.

The best examples are crinoids; the sea-lilies and feather stars. These are abundant as fossils, but their skeletons are seldom found in one piece because they simply fall apart when the animal dies. Quite often their dismembered remains form solid layers of rock known as echinoderm breccia.

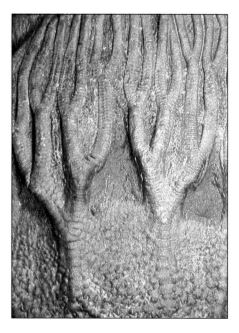

Above: Scyphocrinites. *These are fine examples of crinoids from rocks of the Devonian Period of Africa.*

Below: *This fossil brittlestar, Palaeocoma, shows the typical rigid central body and long crawling arms.*

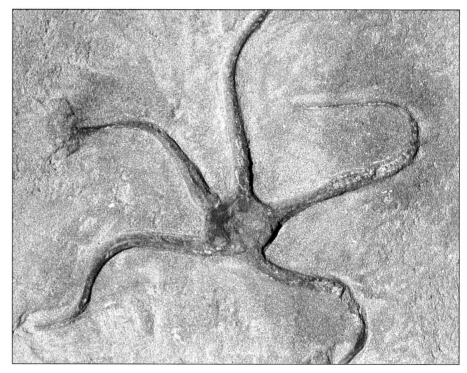

Asterozoans are flattened star-shaped or disk-shaped bodies and, like the crinozoans, have existed since the Ordovician Period. Unlike the crinozoans, the mouth faces downward and the skeleton tends to be flexible (which means that these forms are rather rare as well-preserved skeletons). The group includes the asteroids (true starfish) and ophiuroids (brittlestars), which tend to have longer and more flexible arms, used for rapid locomotion across the sea bed.

Echinozoans can be spherical, heart-shaped, disc-shaped or cucumberlike. None have arms and all are free moving.

Edrioasteroids are sac-shaped or flattened and have the appearance of a calcite block upon which has been cemented a starfish outline. Such forms seem to have been immobile and are quite rare.

Echinoids, or true sea urchins, usually have tubercles covering the body plates, which are the hinge points for movable spines. The mouth faces downward and in many is supported by a special jaw apparatus called Aristotle's Lantern, a frame of calcite, which holds five sharply pointed teeth used to scrape algae from rocks. The regular echonoids lived on the sediment, while the flattened forms were burrowers.

Helicoplacoids are only known from the Early Cambrian and look rather like small rugby balls with spiral markings.

Holothuroids (sea cucumbers) are soft, sausage-shaped objects that seem to date back at least as far as the Ordovician Period. They bear little resemblance to other echinoderms since they have lost much of their calcite armour. The five-fold symmetry can still be seen, but they tend to walk upon a ventral sole (on one side of the body). The remnants of their skeletons are found scattered throughout the body as plates, which are fairly easily identifiable.

Graptolites

Graptolites (found in rocks ranging from the Middle Cabrian to the end of the Carboniferous Period) are among the most unusual of fossils. In outward appearance they look like nothing more than scratch marks left by an old saw on the rocks. Puzzling though these fossils are, they are of great value to palaeontologists for dating rocks that are otherwise devoid of fossil markers; graptolites are widely distributed in marine rocks, and evolved rapidly.

The earliest graptolites, known as dendroids, appear in Cambrian times as much-branched colonies, sometimes joined together by a tubular structure called a stolon, which appears to have been made of chitin. Each of the branches was lined with cups, hence their saw-tooth appearance. The tiny cups, in which the graptolite animals lived are called thecae and the thread joining each cup together was filled by living tissue connecting all of the animals together into a colony. Graptolites seem to have floated in the plankton layer, filtering out microscopic food particles.

Whereas most other animal groups tend to become more varied and complex over time, graptolites show remarkable trends toward simplification of their structure. In the Cambrian Period graptolite colonies were much branched, and the theca tend to be of two types, whereas by Silurian times, colonies had a single strand of thecae.

Some graptolites are exceptionally well preserved, so that it is possible to examine the growth lines of the thecae in which the animals grew. Even though it has not been possible to find the actual creatures that lived in these compartments, it is suspected that they were close relatives of pterobranchs (small tube-dwelling creatures of the sea, with tentacle-covered arms, which feed on microscopic plankton) and distantly related to chordates (see pages 48–9).

Above: *This echinoid shows the typical five-fold pattern of tubefeet (radiating from the middle). These creatures lack arms and are slow-moving algal grazers.*

Right: *This well-preserved graptolite of the Silurian Period,* Monograptus, *is neatly coiled to show the arrangement of small living chambers on a central thread.*

EARLY VERTEBRATES

Along with the pulmonate molluscs and the arthropods, the chordates solved the problems associated with living on land particularly well. The name 'chordate' comes from the creature's possession of a 'notochord' – a stiff rod, which runs along the upper length of these animals, and which is replaced in many chordates by the vertebral column or spine. All chordates also possess gills (at least at some stage in their development), a tubular nervous system (or spinal cord) found just above the notochord, and a closed blood system with some form of muscular region (or 'heart') for pumping the blood.

The precise origin of chordates presents a major problem to palaeontologists. Some believe that they may have arisen as an opportunistic animal – a kind of muscle-powered filter feeder exploiting the rich planktonic 'soup' in the ancient oceans – and it is thought that they may have evolved from the planktonic larvae of other invertebrate groups, such as the pterobranchs or graptolites (see page 47).

Another, more controversial, theory is that they evolved directly from the echinoderms. Some similarities have been noted between the body form of the early irregular homalozoan echinoderms (see page 46) and the lancelets (see below), and it has been proposed that loss of the calcite skeleton of homalozoans and a few adjustments to their 'plumbing' would convert them into ideal early chordates.

Interesting though these ideas may be, they are purely speculative at present. How the early vertebrates evolved is still uncertain and palaeontologists really need more fossil evidence to support these theories.

The chordates include two minor groups – the tunicates (sea squirts and salps) and the acraniates (lancelets), both of which include small, marine filter feeders – and one major group – the craniates (or vertebrates), which comprises the more familiar groups of fish, amphibians, reptiles, birds and mammals.

Tunicates and craniates appear to provide a glimpse of the ancestry of the chordate group and so we will look briefly at these groups first. Craniates are a much larger group and have a much better fossil record.

Tunicates

Most tunicates (the true sea squirts) are stationary animals as adults, living in shallow water attached to rocks, shingle or large algae. They live in tough, jellylike bags and filter out planktonic particles through narrow siphons (their squirters!). Some (the salps) swim in the upper layers of the open sea, living either singly or in colonies and feeding on microscopically small food items. Neither group remotely resembles the craniates in adult form, but the larval young of sea squirts do show some similarities with early chordates. Before they settle as adults, the young larvae are rather like tadpoles; they swim actively in the plankton and have a stiff notochord, gills and a hollow nerve cord on their upper surface; indeed, all the main attributes of a primitive chordate.

Although fossil tunicates are extremely rare in the fossil record, it is thought that the style of life of the larval tunicate would have closely resembled that of the earliest chordate; that is, these early vertebrates would

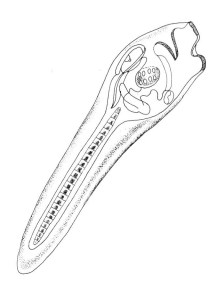

have been free-swimming, filter-feeding organisms with a stiffened, powerfully muscled tail and good nervous coordination.

Acraniates

Acraniates (lancelets) take the story of chordate origins a little further. As adults these animals possess a notochord and, just above this, a nerve cord (which, unlike that of the tunicates, is not hollow), gills, and a closed vascular system (see page 61). They are narrow fishlike creatures, which, despite their beautifully streamlined shape, spend nearly all their time buried in the sea floor, gently filtering food out on their gills.

Until about 1975, palaeontologists could only estimate the age of lancelets and their relevance to chordate origins. It was argued that they might possibly represent an early stage in the origins of craniates – between the sea squirt larvae and the earliest fish. However, several fossil specimens of an unusually slender lancelet-like creature have since been found in the Middle Cambrian Burgess Shales of British Columbia. The creature has been named *Pikaia*, but a definitive account of the 20 or so specimens

has not yet appeared. If this creature is indeed a lancelet, then it pushes back chordate origins to the early Cambrian Period.

Craniates: agnathans

The most primitive craniates are the jawless ones, or the 'agnathans'. The first fragmentary remains of these creatures come from the Late Cambrian Period, but unfortunately, their scales are broken and they are too fragmentary to allow us to say much about them. Silurian rocks from Scotland provide the first partial remains of slender, thinly scaled fish, such as *Jamoytius*. It would appear that this was a small-mouthed fish, which may have strained out food particles on its gills. It may have scraped algae from rocks, or stuck leechlike to the body of other creatures, in the manner of a modern lamprey (one of the few remaining species of jawless fish), cutting out flesh and blood with sharp teeth on its tongue.

Jamoytius, however, was the exception to these early fish, which are often referred to as 'ostracoderms' (meaning 'bony skins') for the simple reason that most were very heavily armour plated. The majority had a large,

flattened, heavy bony plate in the area of the head, perched on top of which were two large eyes, a light sensitive patch (the third eye) in the middle, and a single nostril. The mouth was a slit on the underside of the head shield, and there were small flipperlike fins on the rear margins of the head. The body was encased in large heavy scales, and there was an upturned fin at the tail end.

The pattern of bony armour, and the arrangement of eyes and nostrils, varied from group to group during the Silurian Period and into the Devonian Period, when these fish became particularly abundant. Most were sluggish bottom swimmers, sucking up mud as they swam across the sea bed and straining out the organisms on their gills. A few of these early fish, such as *Jamoytius*, *Pteraspis* and *Birkenia*, the exceptions, were midwater swimmers.

Despite their armour plating, which may have been for protection against the fierce eurypterids – the dominant carnivores of the time, these fish did not survive beyond the late Devonian Period, by which time they had been replaced by more varied types of jawed fish (see pages 50–1).

Above left: *Totally unlike the adult form, these tiny tunicate larva (shown here in cut section) spend some time swimming around searching for a place to transform. The larvae show many vertebrate features.*

Left: *These lancelets* (Branchiostoma) *live much of their lives buried in loose shingle or sand on the sea floor filtering food on their gills, even though they have muscled, streamlined bodies.*

Right: Cephalaspis; *one of many jawless fish of the Devonian Period. Note the armoured head and heavily scaled tail. These were bottom-living fish, straining mud through their gills for food.*

JAWED FISH

Jawed fish filled the ecological niche left by earlier jawless types, and by the Devonian Period were so abundant that this period of Earth history has become known as the 'Age of the fish'.

Acanthodians
The earliest fish with jaws appear in the Late Silurian Period and are called acanthodians. (Their common name is 'spiny sharks', but this is a little confusing as they have very little to do with real sharks.) Acanthodians were slender-bodied fish with thin scales and prominent spines on the sides of the body. These fin spines were the most distinctive feature of these fish and show up very clearly in fossil imprints. Their jaws were long and armed with sharp spikey teeth and the eyes were large and near the front of the snout – typical of a predator. Many were quite small (around 15cm long), but some of those of the later Devonian and Carboniferous Periods reached lengths of eight feet (2.5m) or more. Initially these fish were exclusively marine, but later they invaded fresh water. Acanthodians were completely extinct by the early Permian Period.

Placoderms
Placoderms, a group represented not only by large and fierce predatory types, but also by heavily armoured mud-grubbing sorts, made their appearance in the Devonian Period. The best known bottom-dwellers are generally known as antiarchs, and include fish such as *Bothriolepis* of the late Devonian Period. The front half of the antiarch's body was encased in heavy armour, and it had eyes perched on the top of the head, a ventral slitlike mouth for feeding on the sea floor, and side fins, which were rather like the jointed legs of a crab and may well have been used for creeping across the sea bed. The back half of the body was unarmoured and had a long flexible tail for swimming at speed. These fish seem to have lived a life very similar to that of many agnathans.

The other main group the arthrodires, were midwater predators. Like the antiarchs they had a long, flexible tail for fast swimming and armoured casing over the front half of the body. However, in arthrodires this armour was jointed at the back of the head, so that the head could be tilted up to allow the jaws, lined with huge sharp cutting blades, to open wider. Some of the smaller arthrodires were very likely scavengers, but others, such as the enormous *Dinichthys*, which grew to 30ft(9m) in length, would have been ferocious predators. This group of fish was also destined for extinction; none survived beyond the Carboniferous Period.

Chondrichthyes
(Cartilaginous fish)
These predatory, mostly marine fish are represented in the present day by sharks, rays and rabbit fish. Their skeletons are made not of bone, but of cartilage – a tough gristly material – which is occasionally impregnated with lime to make it stronger. Since there is no bone, these fish are rarely preserved as whole body fossils. The most commonly found fossil remains are their pointed triangular teeth, which are sometimes preserved in large numbers.

Curiously, one of the earliest known cartilaginous fish, *Cladoselache*, is remarkably well preserved. This sharklike creature was about one metre long, and had large, triangular fins. Like the modern shark, it had rows of sharp teeth, but its eyes were larger. Modern sharks have rather small eyes and hunt primarily by their sense of smell.)

The cartilaginous fish have survived right through to the present day, though they do seem to be unable to colonize fresh water.

Osteichthyes
(Bony fish)
There are two main types of bony fish: those with thick fins are known as sarcopterygians (or 'fleshy fins'), those with thin fins as actinopterygians ('ray fins').

Sarcopterygians are of particular interest because, although they are not particularly numerous in the fossil record, they appear to be closely related to land-living vertebrates. It seems that these fish contain a

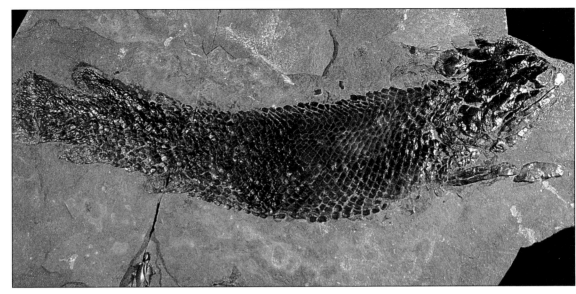

Right: *An example of* Gyroptychius, *a sarcopterygian ('fleshy fin') fish from the Devonian Period of Scotland. This was a powerful, midwater swimming fish with large jaws – undoubtedly a predator.*

Below left: Bothriolepis, *an antiarch placoderm from the seas of the Devonian Period. The heavily armoured head and curious crablike 'arms' suggest that it may have crawled along the sea floor.*

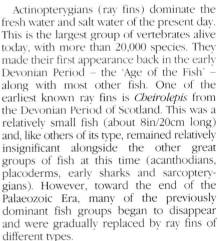

Right: *A modern ray,* Raja. *The remains of this cartilaginous groups of fish (chondrichthyes) are rarely preserved as fossils. Only their teeth are usually found.*

Below: *Preserved shark's teeth, such as this, are quite commonly preserved. Sharks replace their teeth throughout their life, which probably accounts for their abundance as fossils.*

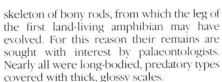

skeleton of bony rods, from which the leg of the first land-living amphibian may have evolved. For this reason their remains are sought with interest by palaeontologists. Nearly all were long-bodied, predatory types covered with thick, glossy scales.

The earliest sarcopterygians are found in the Early Devonian Period and are represented by many species. Most sarcopterygians became rare during the Mesozoic Era, and the ones living today seem to be the remnants of a once varied and widespread group. Living representatives include the lungfishes of South America, Africa and Australia, and the coelacanth, which has only been found at great depth off the Comoro Islands in the Indian Ocean.

Actinopterygians (ray fins) dominate the fresh water and salt water of the present day. This is the largest group of vertebrates alive today, with more than 20,000 species. They made their first appearance back in the early Devonian Period – the 'Age of the Fish' – along with most other fish. One of the earliest known ray fins is *Cheirolepis* from the Devonian Period of Scotland. This was a relatively small fish (about 8in/20cm long) and, like others of its type, remained relatively insignificant alongside the other great groups of fish at this time (acanthodians, placoderms, early sharks and sarcopterygians). However, toward the end of the Palaeozoic Era, many of the previously dominant fish groups began to disappear and were gradually replaced by ray fins of different types.

Like the sarcopterygians, these fish had lungs, but in actinopterygians these were used mainly for buoyancy. They became very well-balanced and adept swimmers, which allowed them to use evasive tactics rather than heavy armour to avoid predators. Their jaws were also modified; the bones were loosened, so that some were able to develop sucking mouths, while others used their jaws for a wide range of diets. Such changes having been made, these fish were able to radiate into a bewildering variety of types, from gigantic predators, such as the five-metre-long *Xiphactinus* of the Cretaceous Period, down to tiny minnowlike forms, such as *Leuciscus*, which was alive later, in the Tertiary Period.

AMPHIBIANS

The earliest known land-living vertebrates were the amphibians, several examples of which have been recovered from the late Devonian of Greenland and the USSR.

Living amphibians are represented by frogs, toads, salamanders, and some curious legless burrowing forms from the tropics called caecilians. All are small, soft skinned and tend to be dependent upon water, and the majority lay soft, jelly-covered eggs, which hatch into water-living larvae ('tadpoles'). These modern amphibians have been called 'Lissamphibians' to distinguish them from most fossil types of amphibian, and their remains can be traced back to froglike fossils from the Early Triassic Period of Malagasy (*Triadobatrachus*). Other good examples of true frogs, with short bodies and long back legs for jumping, are known from Jurassic and Tertiary Period deposits.

The Palaeozoic forebears were rather different from modern amphibians. Many were large, ranging up to five or six metres in length in some extreme examples, many had scaly skin more like that of a reptile, and, apart from a few rare examples, it is impossible to tell whether they laid jelly-covered eggs. Here we will divide the fossil amphibians into two rather informal categories: the labyrinthodonts and the lepospondyls.

Labyrinthodonts

These amphibians derived their name from their teeth; many of them possessed large, tusklike teeth in their jaws, which were constructed of deeply folded layers of enamel and dentine, which served to strengthen

Below: *This small Carboniferous temnospondyl was found in rock used in a dry stone wall in Scotland. In 1989 the earliest reptile known was discovered in a nearby quarry.*

Above: *A remarkably well-preserved frog, Propelodytes, from Messel in West Germany. The fossil record of true frogs is poor because they are such small, delicate creatures.*

Below: *The skull of this labyrinthodont, Megalocephalus, shows the typical long jaw and stout teeth of these early land-living amphibians, from which the group derives its name.*

Right: Seymouria, *a classic advanced amphibian, showing the short body, stout legs, and very large head of these early land-living forms. Clumsy on land, they were adept swimmers.*

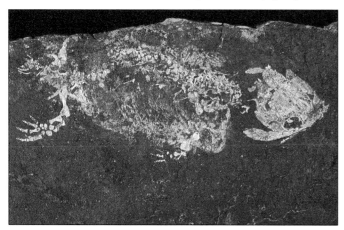

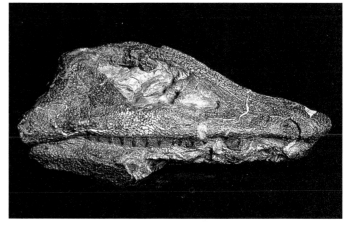

them. Members of this group are mostly large-bodied animals; the earliest amphibians from the late Devonian Period belong to this group, and seem to have reached lengths of about 39in(1m). These particular forms betray their fishy ancestry because they retain parts of the fish-type gill structure, have a fin on the tail and fishlike scales covering parts of the body.

Among the best known of this general group of amphibians were the temnospondyls, which lasted from the Carboniferous Period through to the Cretaceous Period (though most were extinct by the late Permian). They were large, heavy-bodied creatures, often scaley, with large heads and powerful legs. Some seemed to have been large, land-based predators, while others became flattened and more long bodied and may well have been lurking predators, waiting in the shallows to dart, open-mouthed upon unsuspecting prey. A very small number developed long, narrow snouts, typical of fish-eaters, and seem to have taken to living in the sea – a habitat that the majority of amphibians have been unable to conquer. Some very small, salamander-like temnospondyls – the 'branchiosaurs' – have been preserved and show the impressions of feathery external gills. It is thought that at least some of these may have been larval versions of larger temnospondyls, and this would indicate that these forms also laid jelly-covered eggs.

Another group are referred to as 'anthracosaurs'. They are distinguished by differences in the structure of their skull and backbone from temnospondyls, and, while some became equally large aquatic predatory types, others became land animals; either quite large predatory types, or small scuttling forms, not unlike lizards in many respects. The small forms are very interesting from an evolutionary point of view because they probably formed the group from which true reptiles originated.

Lepospondyls
These amphibians, which are distinguished by their distinctively disk-shaped vertebrae, form a mixed group of swamp- and land-living types. Some lacked legs altogether and were probably swamp swimmers; others were salamander-like, while a few were large pond dwellers with unusually broad heads, which may have been used to control their swimming. One group became small and lizardlike (paralleling the temnospondyls), and seem to have fed on arthropods.

REPTILES

Modern reptiles and amphibians are very clearly different from each other; unlike amphibians, reptiles have a dry, scaly skin and lay shelled eggs on land, which hatch as miniature adults. The distinctions are not quite so easily drawn in the fossil record of the two groups because many of the deciding characters do not preserve as well as fossils.

The earliest supposed reptile dates back to the Early Carboniferous Period of Scotland and was first described at the end of 1989. It has not yet been properly classified scientifically, but, like the earliest reptile to have been described before 1989 (*Hylonomus*, from the Late Carboniferous Period of Nova Scotia), it is known to have been a small, lizardlike creature, which probably preyed upon early arthopods.

Fossil reptiles of the Carboniferous Period are relatively rare, probably because many of the rocks of this time were laid down in coal swamp conditions, rather than the upland dry areas where the reptiles preferred to live. By early Permian times, however, reptiles begin to be found in increasing number and variety. Reptiles can be divided into a number of different types, some of which – chelonians, euryapsids and diapsids – we will look at briefly in the next few pages.

Chelonians: turtles and tortoises
Turtles and tortoises are among the oldest living reptiles. The group to which they belong – the 'chelonians' – are distinguished by having a well-developed shell and toothless jaws. They may well have evolved from early reptile forms, such as those described above, but early on evolved armour plating rather than speed as a means to avoid predators. The rigid, bony shell obviously restricted movement and so some types devised different ways of withdrawing the head into the shell (by bending the neck sideways or downwards). However, with the heavy shell to carry around, they were inevitably slow moving on land, so some – the turtles – became aquatic and many types have become adept swimmers in the oceans.

One of the earliest turtles known is *Proganochelys*, which had a shell over 24in(60cm) long and lived during the late Triassic Period of Germany. In the Cretaceous Period a veritable giant turtle appeared, called *Archelon*, which had long paddlelike flippers and a 13ft(4m)-long shell.

Euryapsids
Euryapsids were exclusively aquatic forms and comprised the plesiosaurs – well known for their flippers and long necks (though some, the pliosaurs, had short necks and very large heads), and the ichthyosaurs, streamlined dolphinlike creatures.

Plesiosaurs lived during the Jurassic and Cretaceous Periods, becoming extinct at the end of the latter Period. The long-necked forms probably preyed upon fish and squidlike creatures (belemnites), which were abundant in the seas at these times, while the larger pliosaurs probably filled the ecological niche occupied by the killer whale today, preying on larger creatures, including other plesiosaurs no doubt!

The ichthyosaurs were extremely streamlined creatures that bore strong similarities in body shape to modern-day dolphins (the

main difference being in the tail fluke, which is horizontal in dolphins and was vertical in ichthyosaurs). The long thin snout of these creatures, which was lined with sharp, spiky teeth, indicates that they fed on fish, and belemnites (a diet that has been confirmed by preserved stomach contents). Another interesting feature of these animals is the fact that they did not lay eggs but bore live young. Some female ichthyosaurs have been found with babies preserved inside the body cavity, and one or two have been found with the baby in the process of being born (probably cases of spontaneous abortion following the death of the creature).

Ichthyosaurs have been found in marine rocks dating from the late Triassic Period through the Jurassic (when they were most abundant) to the latter half of the Cretaceous Period, when they became extinct.

Left: *The large conical teeth of the dolphinlike ichthyosaur seems to have fulfilled several functions. Most importantly, they were used to impale fish, belemnites or ammonites, which seem to have been the main food sources of the large swimming reptiles.*

Below: *The fossilized skeleton of the turtle species,* Allaeochelys. *Most remains of chelonians seem to consist of isolated skulls or parts of the shell; it is very rare that both the skull and skeleton are found preserved together as in this example.*

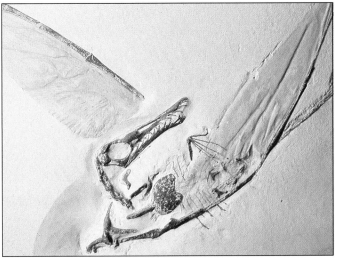

Above:
Rhamphorhynhus. *This is an example of a well preserved skeleton from Bavarian limestone. The fine bones of the skeleton are clearly visible and there is even an indication of the skin covering the wings.*

Left: *Snakes are very rare in the fossil record of reptiles. This example is particularly exceptional; in almost every other instance, snake remains have been restricted to isolated vertebrae.*

Diapsids

Diapsids are among the most successful of all reptiles; the group includes lizards, crocodiles, dinosaurs and birds. They are distinguished primarily by the structure of the skull, the name diapsid referring to the arches of bone that separate two pairs of large openings in the bone of the roof and side of the skull. The earliest form known was a small lizardlike creature from the late Carboniferous Period, *Petrolacosaurus.*

In the next few pages we will look at two important groups of diapsids: lepidosaurs, which comprises lizards and snakes, and archosaurs, a large group that includes crocodiles, pterosaurs, dinosaurs and birds.

Lepidosaurs, the early lizards and snakes, have persisted through the fossil record to the present day. Unfortunately, their small size and fragile bodies, combined with the fact that they prefer dry upland areas, means that the fossil record of most lepidosaurs is not particularly rich. One exception to this is a group known as 'mosasaurs', which were closely related to the present-day lizards monitor. These huge aquatic lizards, some of which grew to lengths of 20ft(6m) or more, have been found in marine rocks of late Cretaceous times. Unfortunately these marine lizards did not survive beyond the end of the Cretaceous Period, suffering the same fate as the plesiosaurs and ichtyosaurs.

Archosaurs are the other important grouping of diapsids, which includes crocodiles, pterosaurs, dinosaurs and birds. The archosaurs were on the whole larger and more aggressive than the lepidosaurs.

The earliest of these creatures dates from the Permian Period and by late Triassic times a variety of early crocodiles had appeared. These were rather small compared with modern ones, and had long legs, so they may have been quite nimble runners on land. During the early Jurassic Period, these gave rise to the more familiar long-bodied, short-legged types that we know today and later, during the Mesozoic Era, one branch of the crocodiles took to the open sea and developed tail fins and very reduced legs that looked more like paddles.

Another very different group of archosaurs appeared in the late Triassic Period: the pterosaurs – the flying reptiles of the Mesozoic Era. They started as very lightly built creatures that may have lived in trees, and from this they took to gliding, and finally flapping flight, using wings formed of their arms and hands, the fourth finger of which was enormously lengthened to support a thin membrane of skin. Because of their lightness and the small size of most, they are rare as fossils. The early ones seem to have had long tails, which were used as rudders, but later ones lost the long tail and became very adept fliers. Pterosaurs became extinct at the end of the Cretaceous Period, but not before they had produced the world's largest ever flying creatures, the 'quetzals', named after the first really big pterosaur discovered: *Quetzalcoatlus* from Texas.

Left: *The skeleton of an ibis-like bird,* Rhynchaeites, *from Messel, West Germany. The detailed preservation of fossils from these reposits in remarkable.*

Right: *This Berlin specimen of* Archaeopteryx *seems to illustrate evolution caught in the act. Like a bird,* Archaeopteryx *has feathers, and yet it also shows a long bony tail, claws on the wings and teeth in the jaws; characteristics of reptiles.*

Below right: *The fossilized head of* Cynognathus – *an advanced, rather doglike carnivorous synapsid.*

Dinosaurs, a very important – and well-known – group of archosaurs, also appeared for the first time during the late Triassic Period. Dinosaurs were at first small (one to two metres long), highly agile carnivorous creatures (for example *Herrerasaurus, Coelophysis*), which appear to have used their hind legs alone for running. Dinosaurs are distinguished from other archosaurs by their ability to walk with their legs tucked beneath the body; all other land-based reptiles were restricted to crawling along the ground with their legs and arms bent so that their belly nearly touched the ground and their feet were spread wide apart. The advantage of this new posture was that it enabled the dinosaurs to run much more efficiently and carry greater weights more easily, which also meant that they could grow larger.

In the Jurassic Period a wide range of dinosaurs, both carnivorous and herbivorous, appeared (for example *Plateosaurus, Dilophosaurus* and *Heterodontosaurus*), and the end of the Period saw some gigantic plant-eating dinosaurs (for example *Brachiosaurus, Apatosaurus,* Diplodocus and *Mamenchisaurus*), which ranged up to 100ft(30m) or more in length and weighed up to 70 tons. In the next period, the Cretaceous, these giant plant-eater were replaced,

for the most part, by a variety of bizarre, smaller dinosaurs (such as ankylosaurs, crested hadrosaurs, and ceratopians), as well as some of the largest carnivores that have ever lived (including *Tyrannosaurus*).

Like many other groups, all the dinosaurs (whose remains, incidentally, have been found on all the continents of the Earth, including Antarctica) became extinct at the close of the Cretaceous Period. However, their nearest relatives – birds – survived.

Birds are distinguished from all other cretures by their possession of feathers. The earliest evidence of birds in the fossil record comes from the skeletons of *Archaeopteryx*, which have been discovered in quarries near Solnhofen in southern Germany. The rocks date to the late Jurassic Period and are so fine grained that skeletons of this creature have been preserved that show even the impression of feathers covering the wings and body in remarkable detail. The first *Archaeopteryx* skeleton was discovered in 1861 and since that time three more good skeletons have been found, along with a few more fragmentary remains. The creature was small (about the size of a pigeon) and unmistakably birdlike with its feather-fringed wings. However, it showed some

remarkable features for a bird; it had sharp pointed teeth in its jaws rather than a horny bill, three fingers on each wing, each with a sharply curved claw (indeed its hands strongly resemble those of small carnivorous dinosaurs). Additionally, its long, birdlike tail, instead of being composed of long flight feathers only, as in modern birds, had a string of tail bones running down the middle, just like that of all reptiles.

Bone-by-bone comparisons of the skeleton of *Archaeopteryx* with other fossil animals suggests that its closest relatives were small carnivorous dinosaurs, and it is now presumed that all birds must be descended from such creatures. It is interesting to think, watching a large bird, especially one that is big and flightless, such as an ostrich, that we may be catching a glimpse of what carnivorous dinosaurs may have been like in life.

Birds, because they are light and fragile, tend to be only rarely preserved as fossils, but their rarity makes them important finds for science. Some toothed birds (such as *Hesperornis* and *Ichthyornis*) are known to have existed in Cretaceous times and some giant carnivorous birds (such as *Phororhacos* and *Diatryma*) lived during early Tertiary times. Jurassic and Cretaceous bird bones are often confused with those of pterosaurs.

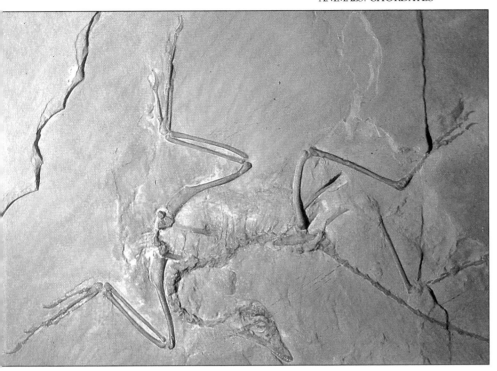

Synapsids

The final group of reptiles we will look at here – the 'synapsids' – were not the last to make their appearance. In fact, their long and important history started in the Late Carboniferous Period – before the arrival of

the dinosaurs. Synapsids are characterized by a particular configuration of bones on the side of the head behind the eye socket, which surround a single opening on either side. (You may remember that the diapsids – the group to which the dinosaurs belong –

had a pair of openings on the top and sides of the skull.) Synapsids are particularly important because they are the group from which mammals are descended, and their history, and that of mammals, is an unusual one, consisting of initial success, a disastrous decline, and then, after a long delay, renewed importance.

The earliest synapsids were lizardlike creatures, little different from the very earliest reptiles (see page 54). However, by early Permain times, this group had produced such notable types as the sail-backed or pelycosaurian reptiles (*Dimetrodon* and *Edaphosaurus*, for example). These were quite large creatures (6.5–10ft/2–3m long). Some were plant-eaters, other meateaters, and many were characterized by a large 'sail' constructed from enormously elongated spine bones. The 'sail' was probably covered by skin, and is thought to have servd as a device for catching the heat of the sun when the animal was cold, or as a radiator for losing heat if it was too hot.

In later Permian times a variety of other types of synapsid appeared. Most had shorter tails than the pelycosaurs and proportionately longer legs, and none of them had 'sails'; this system of temperature control had seemingly gone out of style. Some (such as *gorgonopsians* and *therocephalians*) were savage predatory types with large heads armed with large sabrelike teeth; other (for example *dicynodonts*) abandoned teeth, instead using their turtlelike beaks to browse. By Triassic times the variety of these creatures was great, and in parts of the world their fossils are abundant.

In general the bodies of these creatures were short and compact, their legs were long and their tails short. Many were, in fact, rather doglike in appearance. They also tended to have teeth that were modified to perform different functions; small nipping teeth at the front, large stabbing teeth behind these, and then slicing or grinding teeth at the rear. In fact, by the late Triassic Period these animals were very much like true mammals of the sort we see around today. Then very suddenly this group was almost completely wiped out. A few very small ones remained and these are rarely found as fossils. What happened? We don't really know. But in place of the synapsids there appeared dinosaurs, which became the dominant forms of life on land for the next 150 million years of the Mesozoic Era until their mysterious demise at the end of the Cretaceous Period.

MAMMALS

Late Triassic and early Jurassic survivors of the synapsid group were, so far as we can tell, very early mammals. The tiny – 4–8in(10–20cm)-long – shrewlike creatures (*Megazostrodon*) probably lived nocturnally, feeding on insects and small grubs, just as shrews do today. They had the full range of teeth (incisors, canines, and molars) inherited from their synapsid forebears, but in addition also show evidence of having milk teeth. That is, these creatures were weaned on milk from their mother, as is the case with all mammals. They also had larger brains and seem to have had whiskers (which implies hairy skin) – indeed they possessed all the basic attributes that are associated with mammals.

Such bewhiskered little creatures are found rarely among dinosaur finds. (It is likely that these animals were active at dusk and night when the dinosaurs were asleep.) Most usually it is collections of their tiny (pinhead-sized) teeth that are found in carefully seived samples of clay.

Right: *This remarkably well-preserved skeleton of a nine-metre-long whale was found in Sacaco, Peru. Now a desert, this region once lay on the ocean floor.*

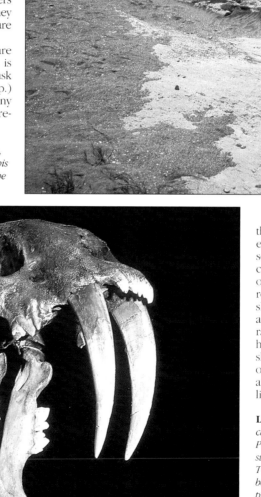

No large mammals are found until after the extinction of the dinosaurs. By then – early in the Tertiary Period – the scene was set for the mammals and they rapidly increased in variety and size to take advantage of all the ecological niches vacated by the reptiles of the Mesozoic Era. Within a very short time, many early ancestors of groups alive today had appeared, including early rabbits, rodents (rats and mice), cloven-hooved animals (the ancient relatives of sheep, goats, pigs and cattle), elephants, odd-toed animals (such as early rhinoceros and horses), carnivores (dog and cat families), early whales, and even bats.

Left: *The sabre-toothed cat,* Smilodon, *of the Pleistocene Epoch (a subdivision of the Tertiary Period) has been extremely well preserved as a complete skeleton in the tar pits of Rancho La Brea in Los Angeles.*

Right: *Many skulls of Man's ancestors have been found at Lake Turkana, Kenya. From left to right:* Australopithecus robustus, Australopithecus africanus, Homo habilis *and* Homo erectus.

Man

The origins of the human species are also intimately associated with the events of the early Tertiary Period, because among the early mammals that evolved at this time were the first tree-dwellers – the earliest ancestors of man. These creatures adapted wonderfully to their tree life; climbing and leaping in trees required good vision and the eyes came to point forward, rather than being on the side of the head. In addition, the sense of smell became less critical to their survival, and so the face became shorter. Climbing and feeding in the trees also provided an opportunity to use the hands for grasping and manipulating food.

By the middle of the Tertiary Period the first true apes (*Proconsul*) appeared. However, it was not until about three million years ago that the rise of the human species from the apes occurs in the fossil record. Fossil remains have been discovered in Africa

(Kenya and Ethiopia) that show early humanlike species (*Australopithecus*), which walked upright. Beautifully preserved tracks of these early humanlike species have been found in Kenya (see page 15) and several partial skeletons have been discovered in rocks that range in age between three million and one million years old. It seems that during this time a variety of early manlike apes appeared on Earth, some large, heavily built creatures (a little like gorillas), others smaller and more nimble (*Homo habilis*). These apes lived on the savannah in social groups, developing primitive weapons and tools from stones.

Between one million and 500,000 years ago a new species appeared that was somewhat taller and more human looking than *Australopithecus*. This has been named *Homo erectus* (upright man) and though first discovered in Java and China, remains of this species have now been found quite

widely across Asia, Europe and Africa. *Homo erectus* was clearly a very successful species; it had a much larger brain than the earlier species, made stone tools, and had discovered the use of fire. By 150,000 years ago descendents of *Homo erectus* appeared that were essentially humans (*Homo sapiens*). In Europe these early men are known as 'Neanderthals', named after the first specimen, which was discovered in the Neander Valley in Germany. This short, broad-faced, heavily built man seems to show signs of being adapted to survive the intense cold of the Ice Ages of the time.

With the retreat of the Ice Ages over the last 50,000 years, the Neanderthal race seems to have been replaced by a lighter built and taller racial type, which has been called 'Cro-Magnon'. This man was no different from humans living today and the last 50,000 years simply trace the evolution of human civilization and culture.

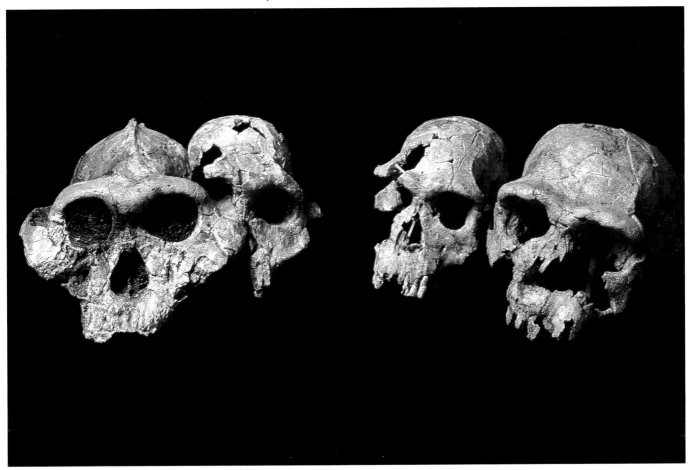

GLOSSARY

A

Acanthodians
Wholly extinct, primitive jawed bony fish with sharklike appearance and prominent fin spines.

Acraniates
Lancelets. Fish-shaped primitive chordates.

Actinopterygians
Fish with thin membranous fins.

Agnathans
Jawless fish, mostly extinct.

Ammonites
Free-swimming marine molluscs that lived in a coiled shell and became extinct in the Cretaceous.

Angiosperms
Flowering plants.

Annelids
Worms; marine and terrestrial.

Anthracosaurs
Reptile-like ancient amphibians.

Antiarchs
Extinct group of heavily armoured bottom-dwelling placoderms with jointed front fins.

Archaean
Early, lifeless Eon of Earth history.

Archaeocyathans
Extinct spongelike organisms of the Palaeozoic.

Archosaurs
The reptile group that includes crocodiles, dinosaurs, pterosaurs and birds.

Arthrodires
Extinct carnivorous placoderms with massive jaws armed with platelike teeth.

Arthropods
Jointed-legged animals (spiders, insects, etc.).

Asteroids
Starfish echinoderms with five thick arms.

Asterozoans
The group of echinoderms that includes the starfish (asteroids) and brittlestars (ophiuroids).

Australopithecine
A type of manlike ape.

B

Barnacles
Marine crustaceans whose larvae settle and grow a plated chamber with a valved lid on top.

Belemnites
Extinct aquatic relatives of the modern squids.

Bennittitalean
A variety of cycad.

Burgess Shale
Rock from British Columbia where very ancient sea-floor fauna is preserved in wonderful detail.

C

Cainozoic
The most recent era of the Phanerozoic Eon, which began 64mya.

Calcite
One of several crystalline forms of chalk.

Cambrian
A period of the Palaeozoic Era: 590-505mya.

Carboniferous
A period of the Palaeozoic Era: 360-286mya.

Cartilage
Tough, translucent skeletal material found on the joint surfaces of land vertebrates.

Cephalopods
Molluscs with a well-developed head (cuttlefish, squids, octopuses, ammonites, belemnites).

Chelicerates
The group to which living scorpions belong.

Chelonians
Turtles and tortoises.

Chert
Glasslike rock formed from solidified silica gel.

Chitin
Tough protein coating that forms the shell of most arthropods.

Chondrichthyes
Jawed fish with cartilaginous skeletons.

Chordates
Members of the group of animals with a notochord or a backbone (includes fish, amphibians, reptiles, mammals and birds).

Coelenterates
Animals with two cell layers and stinging cells.

Conchostracans
Tiny, shrimplike freshwater crustaceans that live in a bivalved shell.

Conulates
Extinct fossil forms, possibly related to jellyfish.

Craniates
Chordates with a clearly defined skull and brain.

Cretaceous
The final period of the Mesozoic Era: 144-64mya.

Crinoids
Seas lilies. Generally stationary and stalked echinoderms with large numbers of feeding arms.

Crinozoans
A group of echinoderms that includes living sea lilies. Some fossil types grew to 20m or more.

Cro-magnon
The earliest fossilized remains of *Homo sapiens*.

Crustaceans
Mostly aquatic arthropods, which breathe with gills (crabs, lobsters and barnacles).

Cycads
Primitive gymnosperms with palmlike leaves.

D

Decapods
Ten-legged crustaceans, eg crabs and lobsters.

Dendroids
Graptolites with a much-branched structure.

Devonian
A period of the Palaeozoic Era: 408-360mya.

Diapsids
Reptile group that includes lizards, snakes, crocodiles, dinosaurs, pterosaurs and birds.

Distillation
Removal of lighter, more volatile elements by heating and pressure.

E

Echinoderms
Marine creatures, most of which have five-fold symmetry, a calcite skeleton, and move by means of tube-feet operated by a water vascular system.

Echinoids
Sea urchins and sand dollars. Echinoderms with a globular or flattened body, sometimes with prominent body spines.

Echinozoans
The group of echinoderms to which both the sea urchins and sea cucumbers belong.

Ediacara fauna
Very ancient fossils of fauna recovered from Ediacara in Australia.

Euryapsids
Extinct aquatic reptiles.

Eurypeterids
Extinct aquatic scorpionlike predators of Palaeozoic freshwater environments.

F

Foraminiferans
Tiny planktonic organisms that live in shells.

G

Gastropods
Molluscs that usually inhabit a shell and move by gliding along on a muscular foot.

Ginkgo
Primitive living gymnosperm tree.

Graptolites
Extinct curious stringlike colonial organisms.

Gymnosperms
Non-flowering vascular plants with naked seeds.

H

Helicoplacoids
Wholly extinct group of spindle-shaped echinoderms with a spiral pattern of plates.

Holothuriods
Sea cucumbers. Echinoderms that have soft, sausage-shaped bodies and live on the sea floor.

Homalozoans
Wholly extinct group of sacklike or one-armed Palaeozoic echinoderms.

Homo erectus
Early type of fossil Man.

Homo sapiens
The human species to which we belong.

Hydrozoans
Colonial coelenterates that live attached to rocks and seaweed.

I

Ichthyosaur
Extinct marine reptile of the Mesozoic Era.

J

Jurassic
Middle period of the Mesozoic Era: 213-144mya.

L

Labyrinthodonts
Wholly extinct amphibians of the Palaeozoic Era.

Lepidosaurs
Reptile group that includes lizards and snakes.

Lepospondyls
An ancient - and wholly extinct - group of generally small, newtlike amphibians.

M

Malacostracans
The crustacean group that includes lobsters, crabs and various shrimps.

Mandibulates
All arthropods with two pairs of antennae; includes crustaceans, myriapods and insects.

Mesozoic
Middle Era of the Phanerozoic Eon: 248-65mya.

Mosasaurs
Wholly extinct giant marine lizards of the late Cretaceous Period.

N

Neanderthal
A large-brained variety of the human species specially adapted for life during the Ice Ages.

Notochord
The stiff, but flexible rod that strengthens the body of some chordates: predecessor of the backbone.

O

Ordovician
A period of the Palaeozoic Era: 505-438mya.

Osteichthyes
Fish with a bony skeleton.

P

Palaeontologist
A person who studies fossil organisms.

Palaeozoic
The most ancient era of the Phanerozoic Eon: 600-248mya.

Permian
A period of the Palaeozoic Era: 286-248mya.

Petrification
The action of turning to stone.

Phanerozoic
The period of time (Era) during which substantial fossil evidence of organisms is to be found.

Photosynthesis
The chemical process by which plants convert sunlight, water and carbon dioxide into sugar.

Placoderms
Wholly extinct ancient jawed fish.

Plesiosaurs
Extinct marine reptiles with four pairs of large flippers, barrel-shaped body and a long neck.

Pliosaurs
Extinct marine reptiles, similar to plesiosaurs, but tend to have short necks and very large heads.

Polyp
Member of a coelenterate or graptolite colony.

Proconsul
Fossil ape from the Tertiary Period.

Proterozoic
Era of Earth history during which only microscopic forms of life existed.

Protistans
Single-celled organisms.

Pterobranchs
Tiny colonial or solitary living marine animals.

Pterosaurs
Ancient flying reptiles of the Mesozoic Era.

Q

Quaternary
The latter part of the Cainozoic Period, which forms the last two million years of Earth history.

Quetzals
Giant pterosaurs of the Late Cretaceous Period.

R

Radioactivity
The product of the spontaneous disintegration of atomic nuclei.

S

Sarcopterygians
Fish with thick muscular fins.

Scyphozoans
Jellyfish.

Silica
The principal constituent of sand.

Silurian
A period of the Palaeozoic Era: 438-408mya.

Sponges
Simple forms of life that seive water through a porous body wall.

Stromatolites
Multi-layered rocks that are remnants of the growth of blue-green algae.

Synapsids
The group to which some reptiles and mammals belong.

T

Taphonomy
The science of reconstructing the circumstances of the death of a fossilized organism.

Tertiary
The part of the Cainozoic Period that excludes the last two million years (see *Quaternary*).

Trace Fossils
Fossil structures that provide indirect evidence of an organism's activities.

Triassic
The first period of the Mesozoic Era: 248-213mya.

Trilobites
Extinct arthopods that mostly scavenged on the sea floor.

Tunicates
Members of the living group of sea squirts that show very chordate-like larvae.

INDEX

Page references set in *italic* type refer to subjects mentioned in illustration captions. **Bold** type indicates primary treatment of a subject.